Patient-Centered Healthcare

Patient-Centered Healthcare
Transforming the Relationship Between Physicians and Patients

Eldo E. Frezza, MD, MBA, FACS

Routledge
Taylor & Francis Group

A PRODUCTIVITY PRESS BOOK

First edition published in 2020
by Routledge/Productivity Press
52 Vanderbilt Avenue, 11th Floor New York, NY 10017
2 Park Square, Milton Park, Abingdon, Oxon OX14 4RN, UK

© 2020 by Taylor & Francis Group, LLC
Routledge/Productivity Press is an imprint of Taylor & Francis Group, an Informa business

No claim to original U.S. Government works

Printed on acid-free paper

International Standard Book Number-13: 978-0-367-14536-1 (Hardback)
International Standard Book Number-13: 978-0-429-03222-6 (eBook)

Library of Congress Cataloging-in-Publication Data

Names: Frezza, Eldo E., author.
Title: Patient-centered healthcare : transforming the relationship between physicians and patients / Eldo Frezza.
Description: Boca Raton : Routledge/Taylor & Francis, 2020. | Includes bibliographical references and index. |
Identifiers: LCCN 2019018218 (print) | LCCN 2019019359 (ebook) | ISBN 9780429032226 (e-Book) | ISBN 9780367145361 (hardback : alk. paper)
Subjects: | MESH: Patient-Centered Care—methods |
Patient Care Management |
Professional-Patient Relations | Patient Participation
Classification: LCC R727.3 (ebook) | LCC R727.3 (print) | NLM W 84.7 |
DDC 362.1—dc23
LC record available at https://lccn.loc.gov/2019018218

**Visit the Taylor & Francis Web site at
http://www.taylorandfrancis.com**

This book is dedicated to all the physicians and patients who have struggled to play their roles. Healthcare is a team effort where both sides of the coin need to be reflected.

A special thanks to my children, Edoardo and Gianmarco: seeing them growing and developing into successful young adults pushes me to be a better person.

Contents

SECTION VI HEALTHCARE CHANGE OF THINKING

About the Author

 **Eldo E. Frezza MD, MBA, FACS,** is the author of the best-selling book *Stay Slim the Italian Way.* Two of his other books, *Medical Ethics* and *The Healthcare Collapse*, were also published by Routledge Press.

He is the author of three essential textbooks on ethics, business, and laparoscopic surgery, and has written numerous articles on clinical practice, research, economics, and ethics.

He has written 10 books and has published more than 200 articles in peer review journals and book chapters. Dr. Frezza started as a journalist before going to medical school and has often been considered a Renaissance man, since his background goes across medical specialties into ethics, business, sociology, and philosophy.

Introduction: The New Healthcare Way

Defining Patient-Centered Care and Theory

Patient-centered care is providing patients valuable care, which is easy to understand and access. It involves all the actions of listening, informing, and involving patients in their care.

To be more patient-centered, health services need to focus on what is most important to patients, by focusing on individual health needs. This cannot be achieved without involving patients in planning and evaluating health services. Only by engaging them can we gain a better experience of care and help patients be more independent.[1]

The Institute of Medicine defines patient-centered care as: *Providing care that is respectful of, and responsive to, individual patient preferences, needs, and values, and ensuring that patient values guide all clinical decisions.*[2]

Define Principles

Researchers from Harvard Medical School, on behalf of The Picker Institute and The Commonwealth Fund, used some

---

[1] Healthinnovationnetwork.com.

[2] www.oneviewhealthcare.com/the-eight-principles-of-patient-centered-care/.

parameters on specific groups to find out what is necessary to patients. They interviewed the following groups:

- Patients with recent, prior hospitalization
- Their family members
- Physicians
- Healthcare providers' staff.

The finding, combined with a review of pertinent literature, defined seven primary principles of patient-centered care. These principles were later expanded to include access to care.

The researchers found that there are certain practices conducive to positive patient experience as they were defined to form Picker's Eight Principles of Patient-Centered Care.

We modified some of the concepts to present the following ten principles:

1. *Respect*: Good care starts with greetings and treats the patient as a person and not as an object
2. *Integrated care*: Coordination of ancillary support services with clinical care helps alleviate patients' feelings of vulnerability and powerlessness during illness
3. *Develop information platform*: Information on clinical status, progress, and prognosis facilitate autonomy, self-care, and health promotion
4. *Comfort level*: This can be established by addressing issues particularly relevant to patients such as pain control, assistance in daily activities, assistance in daily living, and awareness of the hospital and its environment
5. *Anxiety relief*: This can be achieved by particularly paying attention to anxiety over treatment and prognosis, helping the patients get over the impact of the illness on themselves and family, and helping them get over the financial crisis caused by the disease

6. *Circle of support*: This can be provided by making a room available for the family, engaging family and close friends in decision-making, supporting family members and caregivers, and recognizing the needs of family and friends[3]

7. *Continuum of care*: Make the patients understand the details of medications, physical limitations, dietary needs, etc. Have detailed discharge plans. Provide information about access to clinical, social, physical, and financial support. Follow up continuously

8. *Access of care*: The important requirements to provide ambulatory care are access to the location of hospitals, clinics, and physician offices; and availability of transportation

9. *Ease of scheduling appointments*: Availability of appointments when needed

10. *Accessibility to specialists* or specialty services when a referral is made; clear instructions provided on when and how to get referrals.

Causes of Patient Nonadherence

The reasons patients avoid participation in decision-making and are noncompliant with care can be summarized as follows:

■ Denial
■ Depression
■ Dementia
■ Cultural issues
■ Drug abuse
■ Financial cost of treatment.

---

[3] The Eight Principles of Patient-Centered Care Review, www.oneviewhealthcare.com/the-eight-principles-of-patient-centered-care/.

Shift in Thinking

There is a shift in thinking about empowering patients to take an active role in their care plan. The difficulties lie in finding a way to engage patients and understanding if a patient really wants to participate.

Technology is transforming healthcare facilities by helping them to engage patients and significantly improve outcomes.

In this book, we have tried to discuss the most critical issues in patient-centered care and how the healthcare system must adapt. We need to find a way to relieve patient fear by sharing a vision with them and improving scheduling.

We realize that the healthcare system has to make many changes by reframing and improving their process, office flow, and relationship and communications with patients. The goal is to find the true north with a magic compass that directs us all toward the perfect care.

The quest of finding proper placement and of giving an excellent continuum of care both in the acute and chronic situations is all open. Protocols have been built to provide better care in hand hygiene, fall protocols, and more accurate time-out before procedures.

We have to always keep in mind the dignity of each person and respect their autonomy—through transparency, psychological support, and helping the patients to create their circle of support.

We hope to bring attention to a subject, which can lead to better patient care and better physician–patient relationships.

Suggested Reading

Institute of Medicine. Crossing the Quality Chasm: A New Health System for the 21st Century, www.healthaffairs.org/doi/full/10.1377/hlthaff.28.4.w555.

PATIENT FIRST

1

Chapter 1

Patient-Centered Care

Patients as Customers?

Healthcare delivery, since the time of Hippocrates, is
the science of improving the human health condition.
Unfortunately nowadays, the process is becoming so automatic
and mechanical which has resulted in dehumanization of and
disrespect to the people who undergo it, thus ignoring the
basic principles and actual purposes of medicine.

Patients are the only reason for the healthcare to exist.
They are not customers or consumers, but they are people in
need or simply "patients".

Patient-Centered Care

Patient- or person-centered care is an approach in which the
use of healthcare by patients is considered to equal their use
of other social services. Patients are now partners in planning,
developing, and monitoring care to make sure it meets their
needs.

In old days, healthcare was based on a paternalistic relationship between the physician and patients. These days it is

changing toward a partnership where the physician is building a team with the patient, sharing information and vision of care.

Person-centered care requires knowledge of the individual as a whole person. The approach focuses on involving the individual and their family and friends—where appropriate—in helping to assess their own needs and plan their own care.

The ultimate aim of patient-centered care is providing a health service of high quality. Hence, insurance payments are increasingly linked to the scores patients provide on their satisfaction in the questionnaires filled by them, which is really a revolution of thinking in office and hospital practice. The patients are given a voice that counts.

The questionnaires filled by patients have become more critical in assesing the quality of the service provided, and therefore the patients' thoughts and opinions are taking the center stage of decision-making. Patients have been treated as valuable customers, like in any other business, with rights to complain and chances of their payments reimbursed if not content.

Client-Centered Care

In client- and patient-centered healthcare, the physicians are well aware of the moral implications of their work, and they treat their patients as equal and give respect to their patients' thoughts and opinions in decision-making. Patients are known as persons in the context of their social media, such as Facebook, Instagram, and Twitter, and they are listened to, informed, respected, and involved in their care. Their wishes are honored.

God saves all from the wrong report. The questionnaires can be used as a sword by the patients. The patients now have the power to comment on anything and even give a negative report ranging from a cold coffee to a bad relationship, and so on. These issues have been increasing the fear of the physician to discuss in depth the problems faced by the patients on not being 100% satisfied. Such matters are mostly dealt with by customer care. Problems that arise in the form of patient complaints when denied pain medications, patients not wanting to hear the truth about their health, and patients getting offended when informed about the results of their diagnosis can negatively impact the future of healthcare.

Evidence or Services?

The quality-first approach has empowered Centers for Medicare & Medicaid Services (CMS) and insurance companies to control the actual input and output of patients.

There have been concerns that patient-centered care will be centered around individual needs, rather than focusing on the evidence-based approach, which tends to focus on populations and preventions. The proponents of evidence-based medicine now accept that a good outcome must be defined as what is meaningful and valuable to the individual patient. Patient-centered care is both the art and the science of the new evidence-based approach to healthcare.

Even though the final decision is in the hands of the physician and the practitioner, the patient has a say on their care and they can choose. They are more prepared. They can look up the provider. They can access the web pages and read about their diseases and possible treatments.

The past three decades have seen a development of different stages of healthcare: first, patients went to the hospital and sought for help; second, hospitals used marketing strategies to attract patients; and third, nowadays patients browse the web for healthcare services and decide on the best hospitals and physicians.

This environment has helped and empowered patients, and also impacted physician practice and hospital strategies.

Are We Doing Better?

Unfortunately, making healthcare better does not mean making it more expensive. In the name of openness and democracy, we have ordered more labs, X-rays, and more procedures to please patients and receive better web evaluations. But this is not always linked to quality improvement.

Most of the patients are unaware of the differences—they judge and grade their relationships with the physician and the hospital on the basis of the amount of tests and procedures received and not on their quality, since they intend to get all the procedures performed as published on the web. Therefore, physicians and healthcare organizations have been practicing more of legal medicine than real medicine.

Most people are afraid of knowing their deficiency. They are desperate for a solution even though they are past the possible reversal stage of their disease. If not the disease, it is the sense of accomplishment. If a patient is well, they need to have something from the office to justify their visit, such as giving candy to a child or receiving a toothbrush from the dentist.

It is not uncommon to come across a patient going out from a physician's office with some prescription, or cream or antibiotics even if they do not have any infections or pain, so as to avoid patient unsatisfaction.

It is more common to see biopsies and surgeries, entirely explorative, to make the patient happy and at peace in the hospital. We need to work toward a balance wherein the physician takes into account evidence-based medicine as well as patient needs to develop evidence-based questionnaires not only about their disease and progress but also about their feelings so as to achieve a better evaluation that is more fair for all.

Bring Healthcare Digital

One of the positive innovations of the system is the introduction of telemedicine, wherein a patient can be treated by a specialist remotely. The argument is that we physicians lose the feeling, the potential, to look at the patients. The art of medicine is thus missed out.

Therefore, telemedicine can be useful only in a few instances such as critical care, skin cancer, and burns, but it may not be appropriate in situations where the patient has generalized complaints that are difficult to substantiate over a video call.

To establish easy access, healthcare organizations should look at how they make themselves available to patients. Such an option can include an assessment of digital communication strategies, appointment scheduling protocols, office hours, and availability of providers for a visit.

Organization leaders need to, finally, focus on the population they serve and the community they are in. Since the current focus is on the consumer-centric industry, it will be important for healthcare organizations to offer treatment access in ways that are convenient for the patients.[1]

As the healthcare is keep changing due to new incorporations, new ideas, and the rise of innovations, the physicians will be able to offer health services by telehealth or alternative methods for getting patients scheduled through either telemedicine or web online appointment.

Telehealth allows patients to consult providers through videoconferencing, which makes it possible people in difficult locations to reach live physician access and care through telemedicine. This will be the revolution in healthcare in the next 10 years.

Overall, telehealth helps expand access to care for two groups of patients: those in rural areas who live far away from

[1] https://patientengagementhit.com/features/what-providers-should-know-to-improve-patient-access-to-healthcare.

a clinic or hospital, and those who have jam-packed schedules and may not be able to see a doctor during regular office hours.[1]

Lisa Brandenburg and colleagues commented: *"The challenges noted have led some health care leaders to explore new methods to improve scheduling and patient access, including methods of systems engineering and operations management, used successfully in other industries including aerospace, power distribution, and manufacturing. These techniques include Lean, six sigma, and the use of modeling and prediction tools to analyze, improve, and optimize the performance of complex systems, including health care."[2]*

The Next Century

Patient-physician interaction in the next century will be through the internet. The trend will be to get web appointments, consult web doctors, live doctors on skype, brochure, setup protocols, sharing vision and goals with the physician.

A truly free market of insurers and providers, one without financial obligations being pushed to the providers, would allow for self-regulation and patient-driven care.

As long as there are massive financial interests, achieving a wellness situation may be difficult.

These will give patients the best provider and will give the best provider the opportunity to work in an environment that values them rather than devaluing them by the practice of comparing them to a lower level provider.

If a service cannot be provided in the hospital, the provider should not be pushed to do so; they can lose their job. If the provider asks for help in providing a service, for example, in

---

[2] Innovation and Best Practices in Health Care Scheduling Lisa Brandenburg, Gabow P, Steele G, Toussaint J, and Tyson BJ. 2015, National Academy of Sciences, https://nam.edu/wp-content/uploads/2015/06/SchedulingBestPractices.pdf.

performing surgery, it should not be devalued by assigning less and poorly trained personnel. The frustration and suffering of the physicians will only, unfortunately, affect their potential of giving the best care to the patients and will end up in creating a situation of depression, suicide, and so on, currently known as "moral distress".[3,4]

We also need patients to ask what is best for their care and then demand that their insurer or hospital or healthcare system provide it.

For instance, they should be able to request a digital mammogram, an experienced surgeon, timely transfer, or a visit without the distraction of the electronic health record—without the best interest of the business entity (insurer, hospital, healthcare system, or physician) overriding what is best for the patient.[5]

---

[3] Frezza EE. Moral Injury, www.texmed.org/Template.aspx?id=49983.
[4] Frezza EE. *Moral Distress*. Routledge; 2019, in press.
[5] Physicians Aren't 'Burning Out.' They're Suffering from, www.statnews.com/2018/07/26/physicians-not-burning-out-they-are-suffering from moral distress.

Chapter 2

Access to Care

Key to Access Clinical Care

Patients need to be comfortable with their healthcare access to approach physician clinics and providers. Most of the patients are aware of the hospital location but find it difficult to figure out outpatient clinics and various providers. They are unable to differentiate between a provider – for example, whether he/she is a medical doctor or a nurse practitioner – and cannot understand the difference between different physician specialties. The focus of the current chapter is on helping the patients to go to the correct clinic to meet correct doctors or providers to establish their circle within the healthcare system.

One of the main focuses of patient care is on the patients flow at an outpatient clinic. Illustrated in the following diagram are keys to good patient care:

The Institute of Medicine has reported a tsunami of technological advances that are empowering patients to take an active role in their care plan.

Technology has transformed healthcare facilities; helped them to improve outcomes, patient experience, communications, and workflow; and provided them with the technological advantage to deliver real-time patient-centric care through patient portal.[1]

Unfortunately, Brandenburg and colleagues reported that: *Waits occur throughout the continuum of care and are built into and budgeted for within day-to-day operations. The status quo is changing, however, as patient experience becomes linked to provider payment, efficiency and service become differentiators between hospitals and providers, and patient expectations evolve. While excellent clinical care remains the expectation, health care consumers are now seeking health care and support systems that are respectful of individuals.*[2]

They also pointed out that an excellent opportunity to improve the metrics is to assess wait times that measure the

[1] Institute of Medicine. Crossing the Quality Chasm: A New Health System for the 21st Century.

[2] Brandenburg L, Gabow P, Steele G, Toussaint J, and Tyson BJ. Innovation and Best Practices in Health Care Scheduling, https://books.google.com/books/about/Innovation_and_Best_Practices_in_Health.html?id=k004nQAACAAJ

critical components of access, scheduling, and outcomes. The common measure for outpatient appointment wait times currently in use is based on the recommendations for "third next available" (TNA) appointment by the Medical Associations around the country: that is, an organization's goal for its performance with respect to patient access should be to achieve a TNA of 0 for primary care and 2 days for specialty care.[3]

Access to Care Locations

As reported by Centers for Medicare & Medicaid Services (CMS), *"Under the Medicare provider-based rules it is possible for 'one' hospital to have multiple inpatient campuses and outpatient locations. It is not permissible to certify only part of a participating hospital. Psychiatric hospitals that participate in Medicare as a Distinct Part Psychiatric hospital are not required to attend in their entirety."[4]*

Still, according to CMS, *"the following are not considered parts of the hospital and are not to be included in the evaluation of the hospital's compliance:*

- *Components appropriately certified as other kinds of providers or suppliers, i.e., a distinct part Skilled Nursing Facility and separate part Nursing Facility, Home Health Agency, Rural Health Clinic, or Hospice; Excluded residential, custodial, and non-service units not meeting specific definitions in the Social Security Act; and,*
- *Physician offices located in space owned by the hospital but not functioning as hospital outpatient services departments."[4]*

---

[3] IHI. 2015c, https://www.imercer.com/ecommerce/products/healthcare-system-hospital-compensation-suite.

[4] www.cms.gov/Medicare/Provider-Enrollment-and-Certification/CertificationandComplianc/Hospitals.html.

Brandenburg and colleagues reported that[2] ...*despite being considered an essential element of care quality, measurement of wait times, the next appointment or office cycle time is not performed throughout the United States, with little benchmarking data released nationally. In the private sector, their development frequently includes little systematic assessment or improvement. Many scheduling processes have not been designed intentionally and have merely grown in response to internal constraints, resulting in wait time standards and capacities that vary significantly across care facilities. Underlying these problems is the use of a one-size-fits-all rule to wait times and scheduling, the lack of data-driven practices, and the reliance on behavior change to accommodate changes in patient flow. The result is typically a set of scheduling practices that are idiosyncratic down to the provider level and unworkable for the staff charged with following them.*

Lisa Brandenburg continued to report that *It is repeatedly emphasized that the incentives for U.S. health care are misaligned. In the post-acute care environment of a rehabilitation facility, a full census is a priority with few incentives to speed discharge processes. While financial incentives are commonly used at the leadership level, some organizations are now using direct incentives for frontline staff, which offers the opportunity to have additional data and work on process challenges that get in the way of day-to-day high-quality, patient-centered care.*

Offices in Rural Areas

Sara Heat commented that ...*accessing the care needed is critical for these patients to achieve optimal health outcomes. Delays in treatment can result in irreversible disease progression and even, exacerbate the cost of care for both the patient and the health system.*[5] She also pointed out that *Offering*

---

[5] Heat S, What Providers Should Know to Improve Patient Access to Healthcare. https://patientengagementhit.com/features/what-providers-should-know-to-improve-patient-access-to-healthcare.

sufficient access to healthcare services can present numerous challenges, especially in the areas of availability, convenience, and affordability. Offices that only conduct appointments during traditional work hours, for example, may be inaccessible for those who work during those times. Children going to school full-time may also be unable to see pediatricians with limited afternoon or evening availability.

Additionally, patients may face availability issues due to a decreasing of the providers in the area. Patients living in rural areas are the most likely to meet challenges in accessing adequate healthcare. Rural residents often experience barriers to healthcare that limit their ability to get the care they need. In addition to facing the barriers patients across the nations face, those rural living areas are confined due to their locations and a lack of available treatment facilities. Sara Heat then concluded: *through accountable care organizations – a value-based payment model hosted by both public and private healthcare payers – providers face incentives in offering robust patient healthcare access.*

Shortage of Practitioners

The U.S. health system is a provider-centric model, with care delivery defined by standard business hours. Hospitals, clinics, and ambulatory practices are expanding hours and evaluating processes to achieve scheduling flexibility. The current model remains a one-size-fits-all appointment system for child, adult, acute, or chronic patients. This is appropriate for a walk-in at the clinic but not for all specialties clinics.

Plans and strategies need to be in place to define the needs for different physicians required on the basis of their specialties.

With the expansion of Medicaid as in a state like California, there is a continued concern about the shortages of providers' workforce that are now emphasized by the increased care coverage demand after the application of the Affordable Care Act. The Association of American Medical Colleges, the United States, reported that there would be a shortage of more than 130,600 physicians by 2025, without better use of nonphysician providers and staff.[6]

Therefore, we have to face two significant problems, namely physician shortage and clinic redesigning, to reduce inefficiency and boost the office and hospital practices to serve the increasing population in need of healthcare.

Cost of Waiting

Prolonged wait times and access deficiencies also affect providers and staff. Physician burnout is the secondary outcome due to the inefficiency of the system. The physicians become the target of the blame of patients and society, while the real problem, the inefficient system, is not taken into consideration. The corporative organizations are spread across many states that have no attention for local details. A system that works in Tennesse will not work in South Texas or California. Due to lack of administrative support, tasks are assigned to people who have no knowledge about the job they need to perform. The inability of getting things done and the failure of bureaucracy that deals with the system are curtailing the performance of healthcare services.

A possible way to upgrade a clinic is to incorporate e-mail messages of patients, visits arranged through telephone calls, and proactive care activities into their everyday workflow. Improving the best practices by efficient scheduling may help to reduce professional and team frustration and contribute to increase in the joy of being a physician again.

---

[6] AAMC. 2014 Report, https://www.aamc.org/data/workforce/reports/439208/specialtydataandreports.html.

We understand that an appropriate healthcare service program has to face complex issues and has to maintain a balance between clinics and hospital access by understanding patients' acuity and needs. This culture of healthcare cannot be instilled overnight due to the lack of specialists and physicians in a position of managing and decision-making-most of the time we find managers from manufactoring backgrounds making a decision.

We understand that in the United States, the acuity is based on patients coming to the appointment and subsequent decision-making of the providers. We have noticed that patient urgency and scheduling of elective patient visits are rarely found to have impacts on acuity, but mostly it is driven by other factors such as when the patient makes urgent calls, appointment availability, physician templates, and workarounds including overbooking for specific patients and prioritizing referrals from specific doctors, and insurance status.

As Lisa Brandenburg defined, *These constraints add further complexity to an already overburdened scheduling process that is designed primarily to meet the needs of the organization, staff, and providers, which often overshadow the needs of the patient. Despite the national interest in moving to a person-centered model of care, patient and family preference is often a secondary factor, resulting in limited choices, little attention to patient preference, and often prolonged wait times. Insurance coverage, in particular, has been reported to be of crucial importance in the private setting where patients with Medicaid or no insurance coverage have longer wait times.*[7]

7 Bisgaier J, Rhodes KV. 2011, http://ldihealtheconomist.com/media/Limitations_in_Access_to_Dental_and_Medical_Specialty_Care_for_Publicly_Insured_Children.pdf.

Chapter 3

Address Patients' Questions and Needs

Addressing Questions

It is crucial that we address the patients' questions. The two essential points that need to be remembered at all times when practicing patient-focused care:

1. Focus on the outcome
2. Make the patient at ease.

Most of the time patients will have questions regarding the outcomes of their treatment. Some of the questions are the following:

1. Will I be feeling better?
2. Will this disease affect my life?
3. Will I die?
4. Will my quality of life improve?
5. Will you respect my lifestyle and preferences?
6. Will you explain my options again?
7. Will my family be affected by my conditions?
8. Will I have complications?
9. Which options are best for me?

10. How will the implications of a particular therapy affect my family?
11. Will I be able to get a second opinion?[1]

The patients nowadays learn a lot about their diseases by accessing a variety of websites before and after meeting the physician. They can also fill up questionniares which are collected by the system and summarized in different forms; one among them is the Press Ganey score (see Chapter 27).

These comments are essential for the providers to survive by proving their efficiency as these include the quality metrics that can be compared with earlier performances of the same system and performances of other systems. The quality of care they provided to the patient determines the reimbursement from health insurance programs, such as Medicare and Medicaid, which may gain them a bonus in payment or fees for their good performance, or penalties and fines in the case of poor performances.[2]

What Should Physicians Do?

Physicians should pay attention to the patients in the short time they are present in the office. Patients may be nervous and may not be able to express their issues. Therefore, in this chapter, we have put forth few suggestions that can help the physician effectively address questions and doubts of the patients.

Clear Mind

First and foremost, the physicians need to have a clear mind. Take a deep breath. Leave your problems or issues outside the door.

---

[1] Solomon DH. Patient-Centered Care: What Does it Mean for You? https://brighamhealthhub.org/treatment/what-patient-centered-care-means-for-you.

[2] What Makes a Positive Patient Experience? - Ihi Home Page, www.ncbi.nlm.nih.gov/pubmed/3393032.

Listen Carefully without Interrupting

Make sure to introduce yourself. Listen to your patients without interrupting them. Any interruptions might make it difficult for the patients to focus and resume their conversation.

Show That You Care

When they have questions, please listen to them and express interest about their issues. Again, some patients may feel shy, some may be embarrassed to talk about their problems, some may not want to be there, and some others may want to speak but mostly do not. Expressing your interest toward their issues will encourage them to talk to you and explain to you what they actually need.

Encourage Their Participation

Thist is a simple concept, but not all physicians try to do it. Be supportive as though they are part of your team; be close and be encouraging.

Once the patients realize that you are supportive, they would feel more comfortable and be willing to talk.

Investigate Clinical Issues or Complaints

Now it is the time to do your job: investigate the clinical issues, ask why they are in the office or the clinic, and explore their complaints.

Full Physical Examination

Start with the basics and carry out the complete physical examination; evaluate their history and clinical scenarios using laboratory tests such as X-ray.

Make Assessments and Plan

It is not that easy to come to a conclusion when the assessment of clinical issues is not clear-cut. However, when you don't have any idea about the assessment and don't know what to do with the patient's condition, take a deep breath; it is the time of sharing.

Engage Your Patients in Decision-Making

Explain your patients what you think, and share your points of view, assessments, plan of action, and thought process with them.

Follow-Up Questions

Wait for the patients to get back to you, and ask further questions. Note down their questions in detail and pay attention.

Permission to Proceed

Once all the results of your assessment are in agreement, make sure you ask the permission of the patient to proceed with the treatment. Ask if the patients are okay with your plans or they have to consult someone from their family or friends.

Sharing Vision—Patient Participation

Sharing your vision, goals, and clinical plans is essential in encouraging patient participation. Using a team approach and placing everybody on the same level ensure complete participation of the patients.

Patient Focus

The importance of person-focused (rather than disease-focused) treatment in primary care is highlighted by primary care clinicians based on their views of their roles. They appreciate the importance of costs and severity of the condition[3] that is difficult to judge in clinical settings, except in the case of acute conditions. According to Barbara Starfield, *they identify three additional issues: patients' viewpoint of the problem's relative importance, the duration of time over which priorities are set (short or long term), and the level of evidence of benefit in primary care practice. Inherent in a person focus is the notion that attention to patients' problems in the context of their multimorbidity (multiple coexisting diseases) is at least as important as appropriate care for their diagnoses.* The proper primary concern is not the sum of care for particular conditions.

Dr. Starfield then concluded that *Most guidelines that are "evidence-based" have been justified by evidence on "outcomes" that are almost always proxy outcomes measured by laboratory tests. Clinical trials do not identify the nature and extent of the health problems experienced by people participating in them or the extent to which problems experienced by the participants are resolved by the intervention being tested. As a result, "outcomes" do not involve determinations of whether the intervention caused unintended adverse effects, despite the evidence that adverse events are common. Knowledge of these adverse effects is left to voluntary reporting by astute clinicians who look for them. Person focus is not realized when possible adverse events are not systematically recorded and studied.*

---

[3] Starfield B. Is Patient-Centered Care the same as Person-Focused Care? www. jhsph.edu/research/centers-and-institutes/johns-hopkins-primary-care-policy-center/Publications_PDFs/A255.pdf.

Patient-Centered Communication

Many models were devised to understand what is better for patient-centered care. To understand, we summarized some of the most critical points required to be applied by the physicians when meeting patients.

1. Exploring the disease: Physician examines the symptoms, prompts, feelings, ideas, functions, and expectations of the patients
2. Whole person evaluation: Physician explores issues related to life cycle, personality, or life context, including family
3. Finding common ground: Physician describes the problem and the management plan, answers questions about them, and discusses with the patient
4. Procedures described in detail.

Suggested Reading

1. Levenstein JH, McCracken EC, McWhinney IR, Stewart MA, Brown JB. The patient-centered clinical method: I. A model for the doctor-patient interaction in family medicine. *Fam Pract* 1986;3:24–30.
2. Stewart AL, Hays RD, Ware JE. The MOS short-form general health survey. *Med Care* 1988;26:724–35.
3. Brown JB, Weston WW, Stewart MA. Patient-centered interviewing: Part II. *Can Fam Physician* 1989;35:153–57.
4. Stewart M, Brown JB, Donner A, McWhinney IR, Oates J, Weston WW, Jordan J. The impact of patient-centered care on outcomes. *J Fam Pract* 2000;49:796–804.

Chapter 4

Sharing the Vision of Care

Patient-centered care cannot happen without educating the patients. It relies on good two-way communication. When visiting a physician, make sure to ask questions, listen, and communicate what is important to you.

Patient participation is essentail for good outcomes. Patients that do not participate are detached, and they usually abdicate their responsibilities to healthcare providers and expect them to solve their problems. Healthcare is not a magic to be performed only by physicians and providers, but it requires a continuum of attention from the physician, from the institution, but more importantly from the patients themselves to be successful. Corporate medicines cannot change the basic principles—physicians are the drivers of the care—but they can affect how the physicians address the care. Given the fast pace of current health care, there are many initiatives and strategies to help educate patients understand the importance of adhering to medical advice and therapy.

Educating patients with more primary care physicians (PCPs) or providers in health clinics in rural areas is necessary to make the patients realize their rights and duties to be able to get the best care. The process starts with sharing decision-making responsibilities.

Shared decision-making from the National Health System (NHS) in England is reported to be process in which patients work together with clinicians. This process is not always needed unless there is a change in the patient's health. The process results in better coordination between patients and physicians in selection of tests and treatments, management or support of specialist clinics, and identification of new diseases.

The process not only includes medical decisions but also takes into account the individual's informed preferences. Shared decision-making is based on a series of discussions and conversations on the evidence-based information about all reasonable options and the availability of those in the territory or outside the region where the patients live.

The discussion explains all options of the process, including avoidance of the treatment if necessary, as well as the pros and cons and the risks of those treatments. The final decision is then recorded and implemented. If there are more than one option, the preferences of the person are taken into consideration, and the plan is chosen, applied, and followed up based on the preferences.[1]

Practice Implications

According to Weiss and Peters, *shared decision-making tools are a useful way of capturing the presence or absence of specific shared decision-making skills and changes in skills acquisition over time. However, there may be limits in the extent to which the concept of shared decision-making can be measured*

---

[1] www.england.nhs.uk/wp-content/uploads/2017/04/ppp-involving-people-health-care-guidance.pdf.

and that more easily measured skills will be emphasized to the detriment of other crucial shared decision-making skills.[2]

The examination videotapes of participants were evaluated and independently assessed for shared decision-making. This study provides the basis for the potential training and professional assessment to improve competence.[3]

The studies of Siriwardena et al. and Edwards et al. indicated that *The GPs indicated positive attitudes towards involving patients and towards the training interventions. They suggested that the risk information packs were applicable but had used them only occasionally with patients outside the trial. No statistically significant changes were associated with specific interventions regarding doctors' confidence in discussing risk information after the risk communication intervention. Most attitudes and confidence ratings showed positive changes during the course of the trial as a cohort effect. Such positive changes were related to female doctors more than male doctors. Time constraints remained significant throughout the study in not implementing the approach more frequently. Professionals appear receptive to patient involvement, and willing to acquire the relevant skills. Risk communication training did not look to contribute differentially to this.*

Siriwardena wrote: *Practical barriers such as time constraints should probably be addressed with greater priority than the precise content of training or continuing professional development initiatives if 'involvement' is to become a commoner experience for patients in primary care.*[4,5]

---

[2] Weiss MC, Peters TJ. Regulating shared decision making in the consultation: A comparison of the option and informed decision-making instruments. *Patient Educ Couns* 2008;70(1):79–86.

[3] https://bjgp.org/content/56/532/857.

[4] Siriwardena AN, Edwards AG, Campion P, Freeman A, Elwyn G. Involve the patient and pass the MRCGP: Investigating shared decision making in a consulting skills examination using a validated instrument. *Br J Gen Pract* 2006;56(532):857–62.

[5] Légaré F, Turcotte S, Stacey D, Ratté S, Kryworuchko J, Graham ID. Patients' perceptions of sharing in decisions. *Patient* 2012;5(1):1–19.

Involving patients in making decisions is as tricky as communicating the risks. Edwards and Elwyn showed that patients, nurses, and physicians all play their roles in how patients participate in decision-making. Patients participate in decision-making by asking questions, obtaining/providing information, and choosing from/presenting different alternatives. Among the factors that are thought to promote their involvement in making decisions are the patients' activities, the presence of a primary nurse/physician, the encouragement of nurses and physicians to participate, and the treatment of patients as equals. Factors that impact participation in decision-making negatively are patient ignorance, physical and mental imbalance, and shyness on the part of the patient. Primary physicians who tend to treat patients as objects and to fall into a routine due to lack of time were the most unsuccessful ones.[6]

On the other side, Sainio and colleagues realized that *physicians seem to be inclined to treat patients aggressively for little benefit rather than providing supportive care. Both parties seem to prefer to do something actively to maintain a semblance of control over the disease process. Giving treatment, even if aggressive, is a way to avoid the confrontation with the little efficacy that the physician has to offer to incurable cancer patients. This mechanism is reflected in the content of conversations in palliative care. Patient-centered care would imply that patient control and autonomy are enhanced. However, many patients seem to want to avoid information and leave the decisions to be made by their doctors. Physicians, then, follow such wishes while paying more attention to aggressive therapy than to the notion of watchful waiting. This may help to avoid painful confrontation with bad news. Dilemmas then*

---

[6] Edwards A, Elwyn G. Involving patients in decision making and communicating risk: A longitudinal evaluation of doctors' attitudes and confidence during a randomized trial. *J Eval Clin Pract* 2004;10(3):431–7, https://journals.lww.com/cancernursingonline/Citation/2001/06000/ Patient_Participation_in_Decision_Making_About.2.aspx.

remain. Patients wishing to maintain hope and avoid the emotional impact of a full understanding of their prognosis may instead not be informed brusquely about prognosis or the aims of supportive therapy and forced to make an informed decision. By giving more aggressive, maybe even futile, treatment, and withholding supportive care, patients may receive less than "quality end-of-life care." Therefore, information about less intrusive strategies should still be given cautiously, while regarding the patient's defenses respectfully.[7]

Participatory Medicine

Participation in care is essential and has a financial benefit. De Haes and Koedoot discussed that patient participation in decision-making may raise the cost of care. Increasing the involvement of patients in healthcare decision-making may prolong the stays in hospital and increase the cost of care, according to the findings from a new US study. Extrapolating the study's results to the national scale, the researchers concluded that patient participation could cost an extra $8.7 billions a year.[8]

In most studies, factors influencing patient participation consisted of factors associated with healthcare professionals such as doctor–patient relationship, recognition of patient's knowledge, allocation of sufficient time of involvement, and also factors related to patients such as having consciousness, physical and cognitive abilities, and emotional connections, beliefs, values, and their experiences in relation to health services.[9]

---

[7] Sainio C, Eriksson E, Lauri S. Patient participation in decision making about care. *Cancer Nurs* 2001;24(3):172–9.

[8] De Haes H, Koedoot N. Patient-centered decision making in palliative cancer treatment: A world of paradoxes. *Patient Educ Couns* 2003;50(1):43–9.

[9] McCarthy M. *BMJ* 2013;346, doi: 10.1136/bmj.f3597, Published 04 June 2013.

The National Committee for Quality Assurance (NCQA), which established the program, is currently developing a similar plan to recognize specialty practices. It requires physicians be more involved in patient education. It involves a multidisciplinary team approach to care and also includes mental health professionals, nutritionists, pharmacists, and other professional providers.

This is a "big idea," according to Smith and his colleagues, *with profound implications for patient and provider interaction in the future. No longer will the ambulatory care system be based primarily on an "office visit" model. Physicians will be reimbursed for "monitoring" their overall practice population and will receive incentive payments for agreed-upon, desired outcomes. Since payment to providers will not be based solely on office visit charges, there will be greater incentives to communicate in other ways, including phone, email, text messages, and social media.*[10]

The American Academy of Pediatrics introduced the concept of the "medical home" in 1967. The NCQA[11] (www.ncqa. org/) created a certification standard for Patient-Centered Medical Home (PCMH) which was modified in 2011. This list comprises six basic rules:

1. Enhance access and continuity
2. Manage population
3. Plan and manage care
4. Provide self-care support using community resources
5. Track and coordinate care
6. Measure and improve performance.

---

[10] Smith CW, Graedon T, Graedon J, Grohol J. A Model for the Future of Health Care, https://participatorymedicine.org/journal/opinion/commentary/2013/05/16/a-model-for-the-future-of-health-care/.

[11] www.ncqa.org/Portals/0/Newsroom/2011%20ACO%20White%20Paper_4.6.12.pdf.

Chapter 5

Meeting Patients' Expectations and Satisfaction

More and more individuals prefer to be actively involved in their care and expect health professionals to help them achieve the goal. Patient-centered approaches include not only sharing vision as discussed in the previous chapter but also self-management support. Meeting patient expectations enables patients to play a more active role in defining the outcomes that are important to them, deciding the treatment and support that is best for them, and managing their health and care actively.

New studies and research have reported that patients who have the opportunity to make decisions about their treatment and care are more satisfied with their care.[1]

---

[1] https://personcentredcare.health.org.uk/person-centred-care/
overview-of-person-centred-care/why-person-centred-care-important.

Easy Access

The healthcare systems and clinics need to ensure the following steps be followed to create a door-to-door experience:

- Greetings
- Explain what to expect
- Create awareness of the surroundings
- Explain insurance benefits
- Provide comfortable and easy rooms
- Focus on goals
- Share treatments' goals
- Easy referral to a specialist
- Phone call follow-up.

Integrated Care

Patient focus groups and questionnaire feedback showed that patients felt vulnerable in the face of their disease and did not know what to do.

The powerless situations are shared by many patients from their experiences. Those questionnaires identified the areas where the patients felt vulnerable. They suggested more coordination between the following to feel more comfortable:

1. Clinical care
2. Ancillary services, rehabilitation, cardiac care, etc.
3. Support services such as home care and others
4. First-line patient care, such as a clinic or specialty referral.[2]

Reframing the Mind

Reframing or changing an organization is not always for the better, but at least you try to improve it. The bottom line

---

[2] www.oneviewhealthcare.com/the-eight-principles-of-patient-centered-care/.

seems to be how we could better adjust our group or company, in a way that the leadership and strategy are clear and there is a good plan that will be applied to achieve the goal.

Effective clinics and hospitals need multiple tools and must have skilled personnel to use each one of them to match frames to new or old situations. They need to be capable of reframing and allocating responsibility to participate and let staff understand what the strategies and points of view are.

Patients evaluate what they see and not what they cannot see.

The strategy should focus on improving short- and long-term services and access to care, starting with the present situation and looking for continuous improvement daily.

Most systems are revealing only a short-term gain with a short solitary strategy and are hiding the long-term costs and payments that the patient will eventually end up with.

Patients Expect Active Services

The patients expect to have a specific type of service. Their expectations are also secondary to the location. Location can play a major role; having an office in New York is different from having one in a rural area; the expectations and needs are different from each other.

In general, a few things that everybody expects are as follows:

■ No steps
■ No stairs
■ Ramps available
■ Personnel to help
■ Dignity and respect
■ Office line available
■ Hospital line available
■ Daily updates from hospital personnel
■ Updates from office

- Decrease in waiting time to meet staff and doctors
- Awareness of the rounding time in the hospital
- Human kindness
- Dignity and respect.

Communications

Communication in the doctor's office is a hot topic at the moment. As a review by Health Affairs notes, *the quality of physician-patient interactions in primary care has been declining. On the positive side, effective communication is a powerful—albeit underutilized—instrument in healthcare's toolbox. It's associated with higher patient satisfaction, better adherence to medications, lower likelihood of mistakes, and fewer malpractice cases. It even affects patient health outcomes; a review of research concluded that effective physician-patient communication improves patients' emotional health, symptoms, physiologic responses, and pain levels.*[3]

Kasley Killam in this subject made a good point by saying, *In particular, empathy is a critical component of communication that has attracted increasing attention in recent years. Compassion in a clinical context is the physician's ability to understand patients' emotions, which can facilitate more accurate diagnoses and more caring treatment. This differs from sympathy or sharing patients' emotions, which instead can hinder objective diagnoses and effective treatment.*[3]

Empathy is essential for different reasons:

1. It is good for patients
2. It builds trust, thus increasing patient satisfaction and compliance

---

[3] Building Empathy in Healthcare, A Q&A with Dr. Helen Riess of Harvard Medical School about her efforts to nurture empathy among health care workers. BY KASEY KILLAM|OCTOBER 27, 2014. https://greatergood.berkeley.edu/article/item/building_empathy_in_healthcare.

3. It helps to connect on common ground with the physician
4. It aids in better recovery rates
5. It is good for doctors
6. It helps patients to verbalize their emotional concerns outright
7. It assists doctors to acknowledge their patients' concerns
8. It helps doctors do their job well
9. It decreases physician burnout.

Physician Professionalism

A commitment to the patient is not only a contract based on the clinical scenario, but is also for building a relationship. As professionals, we need to be careful as to how we communicate the elements of our message. When people listen, they do not just listen—they interpret. Out of the message, they grab the following percentages:

- Words – 7%
- Tone of the voice – 38%
- Nonverbals – 55%.

It is unfair, but it is the reality we exposed to in our daily life. It is a tough way to gain trust.

The trust can be built differently—first through the message and then through the content and knowledge of the physician. The following are the points of professionalism and trust:

1. Professionalism is related to patient satisfaction
2. Patients are likely to follow through when they trust physicians
3. Patients are more likely to stay with the physician regarded as a professional
4. There is a relationship between physician excellence and professionalism.

The physician has to practice to maintain his level of clinical expertise and personal excellence. The latter requires a daily review of the following:

1. Altruism
2. Accountability
3. Duty
4. Honor and integrity
5. Respect
6. Commitment to lifelong learning.

Patient Satisfaction

A particularly crucial aspect of good patient service is ensuring patient satisfaction. The goal is to create success stories with positive patient outcomes including pleasant experiences in the clinic and the hospital.

We can not underestimate the significance of the first impression. When a patient comes to the clinic or the hospital, their first impression forms from the admitting office; the nurses and the people at the cafeteria can set the right pathway for optimal medical outcomes and decrease lawsuit and complaints.

Not only does a happy and relaxed patient have higher probabilities of being compliant with medical care in the hospital and at home, but making the medical decision also becomes easier to apply and share.

Leaving personal and professional drama out is a must. Patients should be kept away from gossips and problems and even from the issues among the staff members.

Attending your patient when you are distracted, angry, or otherwise in a negative mood is unprofessional because you cannot handle stressful situations or juggle multiple tasks. Take enough time to make yourself calm and free from any negative feelings. Investing a few seconds or minutes in bringing yourself back to a positive mood will save you from many hours of headache.[4]

Caring

The "Language of Caring" is a web page reporting what physicians and providers have to do. As stated on the web page, ... *It is indeed the sweet spot for improving the patient and family experience. When you help physicians and staff build their skills in communicating their empathy, and you inspire them to use these skills consistently to make their caring felt, scores improve on many survey items, even those that appear to have no connection. Communicating caring is a single breakthrough objective with an enormous impact on the patient and family experience. It also strengthens physician and staff satisfaction, because it earns patient trust and cooperation and helps our care teams feel fulfillment from their caring work.*[5]

Suggested Reading

1. Van den Pol-Grevelink A, Jukema JS, Smits CH. Person-centered care and job satisfaction of caregivers in nursing homes: A systematic review of the impact of different forms of person-centered care on various dimensions of job satisfaction. *Int J Geriatr Psychiatry* 2012;27(3):219–29.

---

[4] Solomon M. Eight Ways to Improve Patient Satisfaction, Patient Experience and (By The Way) HCAHPS Scores.

[5] Golde J, Leebov W, Sisneros D. The Language of Caring Programs and Services, www.languageofcaring.com/wp-content/uploads/2017/02/Compassionate-Communication-E-Book.pdf.

2. Gibson PG, Powell H, Coughlan J, Wilson AJ, Abramson M, Haywood P, Bauman A, Hensley MJ, Walters EH. Self-management education and regular practitioner review for adults with asthma, COCRANE REFERENCES, 26 October 1998, www.cochrane.org/CD001117/AIRWAYS_self-management-education-and-regular-practitioner-review-for-adults-with-asthma.

Chapter 6

Fear and Anxiety Relief: Family Care

Many studies have been carried out on reducing the fear of patients while they are in the hospital or even when they visit their doctor, but none of them are conclusive. We have made a list of essential things to be followed by the patients and the office so as to reduce the possible fear of the patients.

For Patients

1. The patients need to know about their disease. The office should assist the patients by exposing them to web pages like Center for the Disease Control (CDC) web, Medical Society, Web Symptoms Check, and so on
2. They ought to be sent a brochure to read at home or a web address to learn from
3. They should know about the doctors before meeting them

4. It is better to avoid dresses that are difficult to take off or any sexual attire while visiting the doctor. Simple and comfortable dresses should be preferred
5. The patients should have a friendly conversations with the physician, rather than treating him as a master.

For the Office

1. The office must have a friendly atmosphere
2. The staff's approach toward the patients should be friendly
3. The staff should maintain professionalism in their approach
4. The office should contact insurance providers to make sure the patients are aware of their claim details
5. The office should have an peaceful environment
6. The internal conflicts between the staff should be avoided to reach the patients
7. The bathrooms and toilets should be clean and free from any bad odors.

Patients should be treated with respect and humanity. Although it is a business interaction, the patients' concerns should be dealt with as humane as possible, rather than considering them as just cases. The Human-Business Model©, created by Shannon and her husband Johnston, provides a simple and brilliant approach: every interaction between the office and the patients should start on a humane or emotional level, then it should gradually move to the business level to keep the revenues beneficial, and finally it should be finished on the humane level.[1]

---

[1] www.plgexperiencesolutions.com/single-post/2017/05/25/
The-Human-Business-Model©-in-Healthcare.

Anxiety of Care

Mary Ennis O'Connor reported: *Fear and anxiety associated with illness can be as debilitating as the physical effects.
As defined by the Institute of Medicine, patient-centered care
attends to the anxiety that accompanies all injury and illness,
whether due to uncertainty, fear of pain, disability or disfigurement, loneliness, financial impact, or the effect of illness on
one's family.*[2]

Turner and Kelly[3] examined the emotional dimensions of
chronic diseases. They concluded that:

■ Psychological relevances of chronic conditions are not
taken into consideration when medical care is given
■ Doctors are trained to pay more attention on biomedical
aspects than on understanding the psychological, social,
and cultural dimensions of illness and health
■ Clinicians can play an essential part in helping their
patients to maintain healthy coping skills.

Psychiatric disorders such as depression, anxiety, and delirium
are common in patients when they realize they have a disease.

The physician needs to identify patients who are at
increased risk for developing anxiety, such as those in
advanced stage of disease; need to undergo specific cancer
treatments; and having uncontrolled physical symptoms, functional limitations, lack of social support, and history of mental
disorder.

Diagnostic assessment and strategies for managing depression, anxiety, delirium, and suicidal ideation need to be in
place to avoid demise for patients in the long term. If this is
not done on time, the issues can grow silently and rapidly,

---

[2] https://powerfulpatients.org/2016/07/21/a-person-centered-approach-to-the-care-
of-chronic-illness/.
[3] Western Journal of Medicine authors, Turner J, Kelly B, *West J Med*
2000;172(2):124–8.

placing stress on the patients and their family, who most of the time acts as a caregiver.

As people are becoming more optimistic about clinical results, patients and their families are more interested in quality-of-life issues, including psychologic well-being and treatment of the psychiatric problems, during and after therapy.

Chemistry between Family and Caregivers

For centuries, family members have provided care and support to each other during times of illness. What makes a family member a "family caregiver"? Who are these caregivers? What does the research tell us about ways to assess the needs of these hidden patients and evidence-based interventions to prevent or reduce potential injury and harm?

Caregivers are hidden patients themselves, with adverse, severe physical and mental health consequences from their physically and emotionally demanding work as caregivers and reduced attention to their health and healthcare.[4]

From the Oregon experience, we learn that family members as caregivers can place their family members as patients at risk. Caregivers do not have the knowledge and skills to perform their work, so they may unintentionally harm their loved ones. Normally, they lack knowledge and competence, which can only be improved through education and practice. Patients have had many adverse outcomes when untrained informal caregivers managed their home enteral nutrition or tube feeding.[5]

---

[4] www.coursehero.com/file/p7buhgd/Research-supporting-this-caregiver-as-client-perspective-focuses-on-ways-to/.

[5] www.atrainceu.com/course/oregon_pain_management_6_units_191.

Aligning Providers and Family

It is of utmost importance that the physician and all teams observe, understand, and ask about the feelings and issues of the family members. More often, the focus is on the patient and we forget about the family.

The family most often feels:

- the notion of "conscience" as an underpinning of his duty to care
- aligned with the sense of duty and responsibility and a sense of guilt
- the need to justify deceiving the person with dementia into believing different things with an intent to help
- reciprocity, by ignoring his previously expressed wishes
- not being appreciated for the strain of caring.

Families living with patients affected by new diseases tend to make many decisions throughout the course of the disease including decisions about care, treatment, participation in research, end-of-life issues, autonomy, and safety.

They do not realize how much care the patient need, and during the late stages of the disease, the caregiving can put even more stress on all of the family members and make a home provider really necessary. The trauma of moving a person to a facility is on both the patient and the family. The decision in the late stages becomes more pressing and more difficult to make, and very few families are not ready. They need to get through, but they tend to keep second-guessing their initial decisions.

Family Care

As cognitive abilities decline, respect for the autonomy of the patient will conflict with the ethical considerations of taking away a person's right to autonomous decision-making.

The problem can only be solved by a sit-down discussion with the family in which the medical and ethical issues are explained. The best will be discussing directly to the patients if they still can understand and share their wishes about life-sustaining treatment.

A healthcare provider must also be trained in taking care of these patients—just showing up to work is not enough. Often, the people that work in these services are not educated and hence are unaware of what the disease can bring. Most of all, they lack compassion.

Personnel in health services need to set to help the family members to cope with any adverse events. Specifically in cases such as loss of spouse by the disease all of a sudden after many years of togetherness, the survivor of the couple may experience significant trauma and he or she may suffer even psychological impairments.

The system needs to be set in the way of understanding what is going on with the patient and their family to cope with any adverse events and to give the best treatment.

All they need at the end of the stages is the dignity of care, which will be our ethical contract with them.

Concern over the Result of Illness

The quality movement focuses on getting "zero defects" on the business side of customer interactions. We cannot forget the fact of the matter that patients are first human beings; hence, we need to balance between the "clinical" and the "humane" parts in every interaction.[6]

From an emotional well-being research conducted recently, it was learnt that: *Psychosocial interventions are increasingly being incorporated into routine medical care, and these approaches seem to be effective. In patients with rheumatoid arthritis, the use of interventions to manage stress has resulted*

---

[6] www.wecreateloyalty.com/human-business-human/.

in significant improvement on measures of helplessness, depen-dency, coping, and pain. Comparatively simple interventions that allow patients with asthma and rheumatoid arthritis to express the psychological impact of their disease and other stress have significantly improved symptoms in these patients. The families of patients who are chronically ill tend to be more depressed and are more likely to have other psychological symptoms. Clinicians should be aware of this hidden morbidity among careers.[7]

The emotional dimensions of chronic conditions have not been considered, and it is very complicated to diagnose both physiological and clinical aspects of the disease at the same time. Doctors do not tend to understand the challenges of the psychological, social, and cultural dimensions of illness and health. But clinicians can play an essential part in helping their patients to maintain healthy coping skills. They need to focus also on the emotional aspects of their work, including how professional development and training can enhance profes-sional satisfaction and patient care, and the critical role that good relationship and additional activities can play in provid-ing balance.

Suggested Reading

1. Pratt C, Schmall V, Wright S. Ethical concerns of family caregiv-ers to dementia patients. *Gerontologist* 1987;27:632–8.
2. Parsons K. The male experience of caregiving for a family member with Alzheimer's disease. *Qual Health Res* 1997;7:391–407.
3. Kitwood T. *Dementia Reconsidered. The Person Comes First.* Buckingham: Open University Press, 1997:91.

---

[7] www.phna.info/emotional-wellbeing.html.

4. Schneider J, Murray J, Banerjee S, Mann A. Eurocare: A cross-national study of co-resident spouse carers for people with Alzheimer's disease: I—factors associated with carer burden. *Int J Geriat Psychiatry* 1999;14:651–61.

5. Fulford KWM. *Moral Theory and Medical Practice.* Cambridge: Cambridge University Press, 1989.

Chapter 7

Engaging Patients

Does Patient Engagement Work?

The Robert Wood Johnson Foundation reported that: *People who are actively engaged in their health care are more likely to stay healthy and manage their conditions by asking their doctors questions about their care, following treatment plans, eating right, exercising, and receiving health screenings and immunizations. Patients without the skills to manage their health care incur costs up to 21 percent higher than patients who are highly engaged in their care. Patient engagement starts by giving patients the tools they need to understand what makes them not healthy. Patients who know how to navigate the health care system often have different perspectives than those who provide their care and can offer insights on how to overcome the barriers that patients face to help improve care.*[1]

---

[1] Robert Wood Johnson Foundation www.pcpcc.org/resource/what-we%E2%80%99re-learning-engaging-patients-improves-health-and-health-care.

Access to Medical Records

Some practices allow patients view the doctors' notes with a technology called OpenNotes, developed at **Beth Israel Deaconess Medical Center**. Also, the Veterans Administration (VA) and 50 health systems in 35 states now share notes with about 12 million patients online, which is a change from print pamphlets and brochures to interactive programs and videos that patients can view online.

According to the patient advisory web, *Sixty-six percent of patients who read doctors notes about themselves felt more in control of their care, felt better prepared for office visits, and had an improved understanding of their health. In 2015, a **Geisinger Health System** study found the software also helped boost medication compliance.*[2]

Role of Engagement

A Health Policy Brief summarizing vital findings on patient engagement published by Julia James in 2013[3] pointed out that: *As a result, many public and private health care organizations are employing strategies to engage better patients, such as educating them about their conditions and involving them more fully in making decisions about their care. "Patient activation" refers to a patient's knowledge, skills, ability, and willingness to manage his or her health and care. "Patient engagement" is a broader concept that combines patient activation with interventions designed to increase activation and promote positive patient behavior, such as obtaining preventive care or exercising regularly. Patient engagement is one strategy*

---

[2] www.advisory.com/daily-briefing/2017/03/01/get-patients-involved.

[3] James J. Patients Engagement. February 2013 issue of *Health Affairs*. www.healthaffairs.org/do/10.1377/hpb20130214.898775/full/.

to achieve the "triple aim" of improved health outcomes, better patient care, and lower costs.[3]

Ms. James continued by underlining: *Recognizing these problems, the 2001 Institute of Medicine report,* Crossing the Quality Chasm: A New Health System for the 21st Century, *called for reforms to achieve a "patient-centered" health care system. The report envisioned a system that provides care that is "respectful of and responsive to individual patient preferences, needs, and values, and ensuring that patient values guide all clinical decisions."*

Involving the Patient

Flower and Levin summarized engagement this way: *Good-quality care requires that procedures, treatments, and tests be not only medically appropriate but also desired by informed patients. Current evidence shows that most medical decisions are made by physicians with little input from patients. This article describes issues surrounding informed patient decision making and the steps necessary to improve the way decisions are made. Creating incentives for providers and health care organizations to inform patients and incorporate patients' goals into decisions is critical. Patient surveys are needed to monitor the quality of decision making. Health information technology can help by collecting information from patients about their symptoms, how well they understand their options, and what is important to them, and sharing that information with providers. We review public and private developments that could facilitate the development of tools and methods to improve patient-centered care.*[4]

[4] Fowler FJ, Levin CA, Sepucha KR. Informing and involving patients to improve the quality of medical decisions. *Health Aff* 2011;30(4), www.healthaffairs.org/doi/full/10.1377/hlthaff.2011.0003.

Patient Engagement

Christine Queally Foisey, President and CEO, MedSafe[5] defined the engagement as follows: *Patient engagement has become a key strategy that refers to the tools and actions taken by patients, caregivers, and healthcare providers to promote informed decision-making and behaviors to facilitate improved health outcomes. The importance of "patient engagement" has been widely researched and discussed with evidence supporting its significance on lowering cost and improving patient outcomes. What is interesting is that amid all of the industry buzz, "patient engagement" is not a revolutionary new concept. In the business world, it is called "consumer engagement." Retailers, banks, and other service-related industries have all been providing their customers with information, tips and other forms of communication attempting to engage their consumers.*

Ms. Foisey also showed a few statistics from Google and Pew Research Center that further support the impact that technology has on patient engagement:

- 4.7 billion daily Google searches
- 1 in 20 Google searches are for health-related information
- 80% of Internet users seek online health information
- 77% of patients used a search before booking an appointment
- 66% of Internet users look online for information about a specific disease or medical problem
- 44% of Internet users look online for information about doctors or other health professionals.

---

[5] www.healthitoutcomes.com/doc/the-importance-of-patient-engagement-and-technology-0001.

Benefits of improved patient engagement include the following:

- Less number of visits to Emergency Depertment (ED)
- Better understanding of the advantages of insurance policies
- Better communication with physician offices
- Direct discussions with physicians
- Increased confidence and clarity of the patient about their treatment plans and goals
- Improved information about health and preventions
- Improved outcomes.

Challenges for Providers

As the trend in healthcare is keep changing, the providers have to adapt to many new changes in their approach.

Providers and healthcare administration must be prepared to face multiple challenges as listed:

- Provide training for new staff
- Understand different languages and religion-based preferences
- Have the ability to explain new or updated technologies
- Implement the new forms and web information
- Educate staff to work toward new goals
- Educate staff and patients to achieve better communication
- Set new web pages and electronic records that are securely protected
- Overcome barriers
- Overcome initial costs
- Apply effective evidence-based methods
- Measure the level of patient engagement.

While healthcare is a field that is still transforming, healthcare providers are the front-runners since they are the only ones capable of performing analyses and measurements concerning engagement activities of their patients.

TEAM APPROACH II

Chapter 8

Building Team Approach and Communications

Increasing Staff Satisfaction and Morale

There has been research showing that offering care in a more person-centered way can bring improved outcomes. Also, this approach has shown to improve job satisfaction, reduce emotional exhaustion, and increase the sense of accomplishment among professionals.[1]

Providing safe healthcare is directly related to creating a team including healthcare providers and patients. Everyone needs to work together with the goal in mind to follow best practices.

The second step is to eliminate barriers within the team and avoid clinically adverse events.

As reported by the Agency for Healthcare Research and Quality, *the aviation industry has long recognized that safety requires crew members to receive specific training in working as a team, in addition to technical training. Several studies have documented poor levels of teamwork in medicine.*

---

[1] https://personcentredcare.health.org.uk/person-centred-care/overview-of-person-centred-care/why-person-centred-care-important.

A classic study that compared perceptions of collaboration between operating room personnel and flight crews found that attending surgeons were significantly less likely to acknowledge fatigue or accept suggestions from junior staff than were pilots.[2]

The same report showed that a growing recognition of the need for teamwork has led to the application of training programs to healthcare settings based on teamwork principles.

Keeping Everyone Aligned

From the *medical synergies report*, we learn that[3] ...*alignment is the collaboration between physicians and their medical groups to share, understand, and work toward accomplishing the shared goal of providing quality care to patients. The idea of aligning physicians with hospitals and health systems has been experimented with since the 1990s. In many cases, those early physician alignment ventures failed to meet expectations, and the idea faded. Then, several years ago, the idea resurfaced. Today, economic changes, new payment models, and demands of further federal health reform all require greater alignment between hospitals and physicians.*

The Patient Protection and Affordable Care Act has made significant changes to the delivery of healthcare. Perhaps the most notable is the transition from a model that reimburses independent physicians on a fee-for-service basis to one where the hospital system employs individual physicians.

Directly employing physicians within a hospital system is one of the main strategies used by healthcare providers to improve physician alignment with the interests of the entire health system. The goals should always be focused on quality patient care.

---

[2] https://psnet.ahrq.gov/primers/primer/8/teamwork-training.
[3] www.medsynergies.com/thought-leadership/physician-alignment-means-patient.

Many physicians nowadays join healthcare systems to focus on patient care, rather than deal with the administrative burden and the skyrocketing cost of private practice. By the end of 2020, less than a third of physicians will be independent in private practice.

The practice for hospitals today is to employ or have a contract with physicians in some way.

The physician-aligned system allows the patients to enjoy improved access and consistent standards of quality throughout the system, from outpatient facilities to hospital inpatient care and services such as rehabilitation and home care.[3]

Where Does Patient Loyalty Come From?

Alex Mangrolia wrote that: ... *almost 48 percent of patients think the most critical time to gain their loyalty is when they make their visit to your office... Brand loyalty is an essential investment for your medical practice, and you must offer value to become invaluable to your patients.*[4]

Acquiring new patients is a continuing challenge for doctors and healthcare providers, but perhaps the most significant problem—with longer term rewards—is the ongoing effort to build trust and loyalty with existing patients. Here are several strategies to engage healthcare consumers and increase patient adherence.[5]

In the past, the idea of patient loyalty in the healthcare industry wasn't necessarily a big priority, if at all. In the present, it is a must because devotion turns to more compliance and adherence of the patient to medical plans.

---

[4] www.practicebuilders.com/blog/the-art-of-patient-loyalty-4-tips-for-building-a-practice-patients-love/.

[5] www.healthcaresuccess.com/blog/doctor-marketing/six-strategies-to-increase-patient-loyalty.html.

The main reason patients stop visiting a healthcare provider is experience of poor service. But what leads a patient to describe a service experience as "poor" or "unacceptable"?

It is astonishing that three-fourths of the decisions are based on the staff behavior and not on the competency and knowledge of the providers or doctors.

Incompetent staff is the most prominent reason to "dislike" a service or service provider.[4]

Teamwork Training

As is the case in other businesses, the new role of healthcare administrator is to train and educate team members to minimize the potential for making errors and respond appropriately to acute situations.

Training for teamwork thus focuses on developing practical communication skills and a more cohesive environment among team members, and on creating an atmosphere in which all personnel feel comfortable speaking up when they suspect a problem.[2]

Team members are trained to cross-check each other's actions, offer assistance when needed, and address errors in a nonjudgmental fashion. Debriefing and providing feedback, especially after critical incidents, are essential components of teamwork training, which in medicine is called *root cause analysis*. These processes help to focus on the cause of the health malfunctions and the steps need to be followed.

Teamwork training takes the following into considerations:

1. The role of human factors—for example, the effects of fatigue, expected or predictable perceptual errors (such as misreading monitors or mishearing instructions)
2. The impact of different management styles and organizational cultures.

Team Safety

The Team Strategies and Tools to Enhance Performance and Patient Safety (TeamSTEPPS) program was developed in collaboration with the United States Department of Defense and Agency for Health Care Research and Quality (AHRQ)[6] to support effective communication and teamwork in healthcare.

TeamSTEPPS has been successfully implemented in a variety of clinical settings, including intensive care units and operating rooms.

The AHRQ offers a comprehensive curriculum and training program, *which includes hands-on training through regular meetings and conferences as well as an online toolkit with an implementation guide, training materials, and measurement tools.*

Initially developed for hospitals, the TeamSTEPPS program has been expanded to include long-term care and primary care. Other examples of teamwork training programs include the Veterans Affairs Medical Team Training program and crew resource management.

Teamwork training programs have been focused on different sections of clinical and nonclinical environments such as the emergency department, operating rooms, obstetrics units, and outpatient primary care clinics but not on the security section. The security now is attracting more attention from the hospitals. More online modules and trainings are offered to the staff including one-on-one staff training on how to avoid aggressive patients and how to defend oneself from them in hospital environment. These pieces of training are mandatory. It has become compulsory to train hospital administrators as well.

The evidence supporting the benefits of such programs in healthcare is growing. Studies have consistently demonstrated improvements in participants' knowledge of teamwork principles, attitudes toward the importance of teamwork, and overall

---

[6] www.ahrq.gov/.

safety climate, although these have not necessarily translated into permanent behavioral changes or enhanced skills.

Despite the success of introducing the concept of teamwork training programs, they will not be successful if a base of communications is not set as fundamental to improve and select the teamwork. The structure of communication is based on the SBAR (situation, background, assessment, recommendation) technique.

SBAR: Situation, Background, Assessment, Recommendation

The team leader should identify the roles of each member and understand their limitations. Team spirit should be built and maintained. Training for skill development should be made available. Essential equipment should be made available for the hospital teams. Monitoring of safety measures should be implemented.

Communications between Healthcare Teams

Effective communication is characterized by a common purpose and intent and collaboration. Team members value familiarity over formality. Healthcare team members need to trust and cooperate with each other to achieve a common goal, providing the best care possible for their patients.

With the increased demands on the healthcare providers, staff, and teams, there is likely to be a gap and disconnect between the healthcare staff of different domains. To overcome this problem, we need to identify our roles, leadership, accountability, and proper staffing and ensure providing the right training that defines the roles and responsibilities of each member of the team. There should be checks and double checks, accountable members, adequate supervision, and training for supervisors. Equipment should be made available and be in line with those available in similar institutions. The team needs to learn how to operate them. The staff should not just be recruited to fill the positions in the system, they should also be trained personnel. Above all, it is not just healthcare but an outstanding health care what we all strive for. Huddles, codes training, and code of conduct should be a regular practice. Moral of the team needs to be addressed in addition to frustrations and concerns. Team leaders should be respected and their instructions be followed.

The physician should assess the situation and make recommendations. The following technique should be used for the assessment of issues in the task:

STICC: Situation Task Intent Concern Calibrate

This is a structured briefing protocol, used by firefighters. It is based on five steps:

1. SITUATION: This is what I think we face
2. TASK: This is what I think we should do
3. INTENT: Here is why
4. CONCERNS: This is what we should keep our eyes on
5. CALIBRATE: Talk to me. Tell me if you don't understand, can't do it, or know something I do not.

Chapter 9

Common Ground with the Patients

Better Quality

Medical quality is the degree to which healthcare systems, services, and supplies for individuals and populations increase the likelihood of positive health outcomes and are consistent with current professional knowledge.

Clinical quality improvement is an interdisciplinary process designed to raise the standards of the delivery of preventive, diagnostic, therapeutic, and rehabilitative measures to maintain, restore, or improve the health outcomes of individuals and populations.[1]

Phillip Caper has defined medical quality as: *The quality of medical care rendered by physicians in and outside of hospitals has become a subject of increasing public and, more recently, private-sector concern. Until quite recently, third-party payers were reluctant to question the medical decisions of physicians, recognizing that medicine is a complex equation and that one of the hallmarks of a profession is self-regulation.*

---

[1] www.radiationoncology.com.au/providing-a-quality-radiation-oncology-service/introduction/.

Beyond the issue of professional autonomy, though, is the reality that "quality" is defined differently by different interests. Philip Caper has also discussed the evolution of federal involvement in the pursuit of quality, noting that organized medicine has never been bashful about employing the quality argument to thwart health policy thrusts that it opposed.[2]

Better Quality Equals Better Care

How can we provide better care and professionalism?

Quality is the tool through which both professionalism and relationship a physician with patients and another physician are measured. To maintain quality, care needs to be provided according to basic standards, which is based on the following:

1. Improving the quality of care
2. Improving access to care
3. Fair distribution of present resources
4. Commitment to scientific knowledge
5. Maintaining trust by managing conflicts of interest
6. Commitment to professional responsibilities.

Explanation of Treatment Goals

Dr Fred Kleisinger suggested ensuring that the physician and the patient have a shared understanding of the importance of the medical problem in question, the availability of adequate treatments for this issue, and the risks if the problem remains untreated or undertreated.

This shared understanding is the foundation on which all treatment contracts are based. Start by asking how the patient understands the medical condition and why it needs treatment.

---

[2] www.healthaffairs.org/doi/full/10.1377/hlthaff.7.1.49.

Ask if the patient has any concerns or questions about the recommended procedures, lifestyle modifications, diagnostic tests, or follow-up and monitoring plans.[3]

Make sure you have a connection with your patients. Make sure you ask your patients if they have done anything used in the past is fair game if it was successful in their treatment. Make sure that the patients given enough time to think. Then, tailor your approach in such a way that the patients follow you. It will help in improving healthcare compliance.

Ask the patient for his or her analysis of the roots of the problems. Dr Fred Kleisinger found below open-ended, non-judgmental questions as very useful:

"What can we do to help?"
"How could we solve this problem?"
"Do we have any obstacles to deal with and which ones are those?"

Asking a question with an open problem-solving attitude can make a significant impact on your relationship with the patient and make the patient comfortable and open to suggestions.

Questions to Ask

Please describe in your own words how you understand your medical disorder.

Do you know the purpose of the treatment and the consequences of ineffective therapy?

Please could you summarize the recommendation we talked about and we agreed upon?

Work to mutually find solutions which you can agreed upon.

---

[3] Kleisinger F. Working with the Noncompliant Patient. (n.d.). www.thepermanente-journal.org/issues/2004/summer/51-the-permanente-journal.

AMA Focus Training

There are training sessions offered by the American Medical Association (AMA)[4] and other organizations, but we would like to suggest more focused and real-time training on below aspects:

1. Advanced Communication Skills for Physicians
2. Admitting Mistakes: Ethics and Communication
3. Working Across Language and Cultures: The Case for Informed Consent
4. Working with Professionals Around You: Team Communication
5. How to Deliver a Bad News
6. Physicians' Experience of Stress in Practicing Medicine.

The specific educational goals and objectives of these training[5] are as follows:

1. Building a good relationship
2. Educating patients and sharing information about the disease with them
3. Learning the relevant ethical constructs underlying informed consent
4. Deciding on what to do
5. Teaching communication skills to patients and colleagues, defining our personal and professional goals, and sharing the experience of living in an inexact profession where perfection is a worthy—but unachievable—goal but is the challenge to achieve professionalism

---

[4] https://healthcarecomm.org/training/faculty-courses/clinician-patient-communication/.

[5] www.healthaffairs.org/doi/full/10.1377/hlthaff.2009.0450.

6. Having the courage to face these challenges in open forums with residents, junior faculty, and senior faculty, which is not only a requirement of the medical accrediting agencies but also the right thing to do.

Recently, honest attempts to coordinate the care of patients with complex healthcare needs have further stressed the patient confidentiality to the breaking point. Internet programs now permit wide access to a patient's medical record. The clear benefit to the patient and the treating physician is to guarantee accurate retrieval and assessment of each patient's medications, allergies, and medical history.

People Negotiation

Negotiations are fundamental and critical to the patient's engagement. These are not likely to make much progress as long as one side believes that the fulfillment of their basic human needs is being trampled by the other. There are usually four significant obstacles:

1. Premature judgment
2. Searching for a single answer
3. Assumption of a solution
4. Assuming that solving the problem resolves the issue.

If you sit at a negotiation table and do not understand the four obstacles of the other side, you probably will never be able to explain your situation. I learned that to reach an agreement in a negotiation, you need to develop a solution that also appeals to the self-interest of the other. Therefore, one lesson that I will apply for my next negotiation is to be prepared and be ready with creative options to broaden the opportunity on the table, rather than look for a single answer.

The next thing is to generate possible "YAIS" below steps should be followed:

1. Make strategies
2. Have alternate actions if no agreement is reached
3. Improve some of the ideas and convert them into practical alternatives
4. Select one alternative that seems the best.

You should also think about the alternatives to a negotiating agreement available to the other side. I will consider the following three steps, which I defined as "doubleR Q" in negotiating and rules of bargaining where the other side seems to be using tricky tactics.

1. Recognize the tactics
2. Raise the issue explicitly
3. Question the tactics legitimately and to the best of your ability, and negotiate it.

Suggested Reading

1. Caper P. The meaning of quality in medical care. *N Engl J Med* 1974;291:1136–7.
2. Agency for Health Care Policy and Quality. www.ahrq.gov/professionals/quality-patient-safety/talkingquality/create/sixdomains.html.
3. American College Medical Quality: Policies. www.acmq.org/policies/policies1and2.pdf.
4. Klinger and Medical Condition. https://books.google.com/books?id=PJ4oDQAAQBAJ&pg=PA986&lpg=PA986&dq=Kleisinger-+AND+MEDICAL+QUALITY&source=bl&ots=PYVh6vu8HD&sig=DM9-oRSulPg7z65oryOuWt70xBE&hl=en&sa=X&ved=0ahUKEwjImsrZn57ZAhVOJKwKHdG7Bj0Q6AEIPTAD#v=onepage&q=Kleisinger%20AND%20MEDICAL%20QUALITY&f=false.

5. Klinger and Medical Quality. https://books.google.com/books?
id=wBa5BgAAQBAJ&pg=PA67&lpg=PA67&dq=Kleisinger+AND
+MEDICAL+QUALITY&source=bl&ots=9JTJ66kjLB&sig=3vXXm
Hydfo_vRlfsmmQeoEcVpUU&hl=en&sa=X&ved=0ahUKEwjIms
rZn57ZAhVOJKwKHdG7Bj0Q6AEIQjAF#v=onepage&q=Kleisin
ger%20AND%20MEDICAL%20QUALITY&f=false.
6. Agency for Health Care Policy and Quality. www.ahrq.gov/
professionals/quality-patient-safety/quality-resources/tools/
chtoolbx/understand/index.html.
7. Stanford Health Care. https://stanfordhealthcare.org/about-us/
quality.html.
8. Claxton G, Cox C, Gonzales S, Kamal R, Levitt L.
Kaiser Family Foundation; Measuring the Quality of
Healthcare in the U.S., www.healthsystemtracker.org/brief/
measuring-the-quality-of-healthcare-in-the-u-s/.

Chapter 10

Confusion over Care

The first thing the patients wish to know is how the physician will "fix" their problems. Some patients are so eager to know about their health status, so they will start asking questions from the bottom and ask right away the last question first.

It is difficult for physicians to answer such questions at early stages because they need sufficient time to evaluate the patient's health conditions by asking questions about symptoms, signs, and so on.

Here, the physician plays the role of a detective, who first tries to collect all evidence and proof, and then goes after the "criminal."

"Doc, can you fix it?"; "Will I survive?"; "Do I need to die?"

Sometimes patients might become aggressive toward the physician due to intense emotional stress when their health status is negative.

But the patient is a patient because they are in need of a treatment. Therefore, the patient should focus only on their requirement and make sure they understand the goal of this interaction.

This is similar to a business interaction where the patient is the consumer who comes for treatment and the physician is the provider who gives the medicine.

The only problem at time is that the patients need to adhere to the treatment plans which demand additional efforts. Some patients may not show interest in making any efforts; they think they can get away with *murdering their body without any side effect*, but they need to understand that to get better, they have to be wholly involved in the treatment.

Where Does the Confusion Come From?

If the patient is confused, where does the confusion usually come from? We will try to address some of the causes of confusion.

Poor Communication

Sometimes patients receive wrong or unnecessary information from the people around them, such as friends, family, other physicians, or healthcare providers, which may increase their worry.

In my experience, people around the patients simply dump them with unnecessary details. I have come across an emergency room (ER) physician giving information about the surgery to the patient instead of leaving it to the surgeon to explain the disease and the surgical treatment. Therefore, when I discussed with the patients, they were all over me because they thought I was wrong.

It took quite a while for me to convince them that I was the surgeon and what I was doing was correct, and the ER physician was not a surgeon and would not perform the surgery, and that his plan of action was not appropriate.

This can create conflicts with your patients even before you start the treatment.

Physicians and healthcare providers should avoid interfering in other physicians' specialties and limit their suggestions within their roles and specialities.

Another prevailing instance is that a patient comes to your clinic and informs about "their doctor's" instructions regarding their surgery. It takes a lot to change this kind of patients' mindset about the specific procedure, since they trust their primary doctor but they don't understand that he or she is not a surgeon and they should leave the surgery decision to you. It is like starting a game with a penalty. A primary care physician (PCP) should not do that because that creates confusion and may possibly lead to lawsuit.

Unrealistic Expectations

It is difficult to disclose to the patient that they can live only a short period of time, or they need to undergo chemotherapy, or they need a surgery and the surgery is complicated.

The patient believes that a physician can make them better. Physicians are not magicians, and it is important to make the patients understand this right away. Only God can make them new; physicians can only help and fix some problems.

The web search is also a problem because the information obtained may not be appropriate; there are both useful and wrong information available in Internet. Information from all web pages and YouTube may not always be correct and sometimes come from people without proper training and experience. The patient needs to identify the right things to follow and should have a realistic expectation. Because once they set their mind, it is very difficult to change their mindset.

Different Levels of Education

Nowadays educating a patient has become more difficult, because the paternalistic approach can no longer be followed. Even ordinary patients want to know everything about their treatment and prefer to take their own decisions.

It is difficult to explain clinical issues to patients even if you try to make it accessible in an original and understandable language.

Socioeconomic Issues

It is easy to talk to patients that do not depend on insurances and co-payments since they are more open to plans of actions.

When the patient is economically weak to support the treatment, the physician should consider it and make a plan that works for them.

Here is an example. In my practice, when I do a colonoscopy, I order two bottle preps with drinks and suppository to avoid drinking the gallon preparation.

These bottle preps, even if not expensive, cost more than the gallon prep, but some patients can only afford Golytely as it costs less.

On the antibiotics side, there are many new varieties in the market. The quinolones (Levoquin@) cost more than the old Trimethoprim sulfa (Bactrim@). Therefore, I noticed that if I prescribe the latter, there is 100% adherence to the therapy. If I prescribe the former, there is around 30% dropout from the treatment.

This example is not to instruct the physicians on how to practice, but to ensure that they consider the economical ability of the patient.

Past Experience

It is essential during the interview to ask the patients if they have ever been hospitalized or if they have had other physicians. If the physician suspects that the patient had a bad previous experience with the healthcare system, it is imperative to remove first the bad impression of the patient on the system.

Only by refreshing their mind, the patient will be open to your decisions and will accept and follow your clinical plans and goals and adhere to the treatment.

We need to understand those issues—it could be as simple as a lousy relationship with some personnel.

If their bad experience was with the physician, try your best to gain their respects and adherence.

Abusing the Healthcare System

Abuse of the system by some of the patients is quite common nowadays.

The chronic disease or the abuse of the emergency room is manifesting in front of our eyes.

It is imperative, therefore, that we try to rewrite the patient's mind and way of thinking. We need to encourage the patients to use our office and follow our plans, and we should be available if they need us with a quick booking of a new appointment.

The best action is to follow a strategy and not deviate from it.

Patients Ruined for Other Patients

Mrs. H was an average woman living in an ordinary town in the United States. The small town mentality, I guess. She took her 25-year-old son to the emergency room with acute abdominal pain, suspecting appendicitis. The emergency room doctor did something that is a no-no in other physicians' point of view. He told the patient what the surgeon was going to do. The surgeon, however, did not work in the emergency room, and the physician would not have known what the surgeon would find. He shouldn't have said anything.

The surgery was successful, and the patient recovered without any problems. Clinically, medically, and surgically, the treatment was a total success.

The surgeon later was informed that multiple complaints had been filed against him. He was pushy to the nurse that night, according to the patient's mother. He was "screaming" on his cell phone in a public space at another point in the evening. The surgeon was reprimanded because this one woman was not comfortable with what he was doing when she was highly agitated herself.

Mrs. H did not see that the nurse was not actively involved in her job and that her son's well-being could have been jeopardized by such laziness. Mrs. H never stopped to think that the cell phone call she witnessed was a private one in a nonclinical area and had absolutely nothing to do with her son's treatment, as the surgery by that time had been completed. It never occurred to her that the surgeon was advocating for her son in the first incident and that the second incident was in no way her business.

Hospitals and clinics in the United States are terrified of lawsuits and will bite the hand that feeds them to avoid one. She returned to meet the surgeon later during a follow-up visit with her son. The surgeon hoped to make her understand his side of things. She wasn't having any of it. Any argument he offered, she had an excuse for. She was pleased with his surgical skills and her son's recovery; it was just these two things that she did not see in their fullness that she had to defend no matter what.

Her two meritless complaints were two steps toward the surgeon leaving that hospital. He was an excellent surgeon; he still is. But when stupid complaints of such nature were taken seriously by the powers, it made the surgeon leave the little town. Now patients need an extra $70,000 on their medical bill to be airlifted elsewhere to get the surgery done. Maybe if the patients who are paying this bill come to know the reason, they will be very upset with Mrs. H. She had her victory, and all the others lost. In the meantime, other sons and daughters will suffer and will have to be transported away, thanks to her selfish stupidity.

Suggested Reading

1. Committee on Quality of Health Care in America. *Institute of Medicine. Crossing the Quality Chasm: A New Health System for the 21st Century.* Washington, DC: National Academy Press; 2001.
2. Rogers CR. The characteristics of a helping relationship. In: Rogers CR, ed. *On Becoming a Person: A Therapist's View of Psychotherapy.* Boston, MA: Houghton Mifflin; 1961;39–58.
3. McWhinney IR. Patient-centered and doctor-centered models of clinical decision making. In: Sheldon M, Brook J, Rector A, eds. *Decision Making in General Practice.* London: Stockton; 1985;31–46.
4. Gerteis M, Edgeman-Levitan S, Daley J, Delbanco T. *Through the Patient's Eyes: Understanding and Promoting Patient-Centered Care,* 1st edn. San Francisco, CA: Jossey-Bass; 1993.
5. Balint M. *The Doctor, his Patient, and the Illness.* New York, NY: International Universities Press; 1957.
6. Entralgo PL. *Doctor and Patient.* New York, NY: McGraw-Hill Book Company; 1969.
7. Guyatt G, Montori V, Devereaux PJ, Schünemann H, Bhandari M. Patients at the center: In our practice, and our use of language. *ACP J Club* 2004;140(1):A11–2.
8. McWhinney IR. An acquaintance with particulars.... *Fam Med* 1989;21(4):296–8.
9. Epstein RM, Street RL Jr. *Patient-Centered Communication in Cancer Care: Promoting Healing and Reducing Suffering.* Bethesda, MD: National Cancer Institute, NIH; 2007.
10. Epstein RM, Fiscella K, Lesser CS, Stange KC. Why the nation needs a policy push on patient-centered health care. *Health Aff (Millwood)* 2010;29(8):1489–95.
11. Epstein RM, Franks P, Fiscella K, Shields CG, Meldrum SC, Kravitz RL, Duberstein PR Measuring patient-centered communication in patient-physician consultations: Theoretical and practical issues. *Soc Sci Med* 2005;61(7):1516–28.

12. Epstein RM, Peters E. Beyond information: Exploring patients' preferences. *JAMA*. 2009;302(2):195–7.

13. Hudon C, Fortin M, Haggerty JL, Lambert M, Poitras M-E. Measuring patient perceptions of patient-centered care: A systematic review of tools for family medicine. *Ann Fam Med* 2011;9(2):155–64.

14. Kinmonth AL, Woodcock A, Griffin S, Spiegal N, Campbell MJ. The diabetes care from diagnosis research team. A randomized controlled trial of patient-centered care of diabetes in general practice: Impact on current wellbeing and future disease risk. *BMJ*. 1998;317(7167):1202–8.

15. Street RL Jr, Makoul G, Arora NK, Epstein RM. How does communication heal? Pathways linking clinician-patient communication to health outcomes. *Patient Educ Couns*. 2009;74(3):295–301.

16. Arora NK, Weaver KE, Clayman ML, Oakley-Girvan I, Potosky AL. Physicians' decision-making style and psychosocial outcomes among cancer survivors. *Patient Educ Couns*. 2009;77(3):404–12.

Chapter 11

Coordinating Patients' Participation

Coordination of Care

Patient care has different faces; it depends on whether the care is given in the hospital, in the clinic, or in the emergency room.

Emergency room care is quite clear—the patient has an acute issue and needs a solution right then and there. In the clinic, instead, patients come to discuss problems and try to find a long-term solution.

Hospital care can also be divided into acute issues such as those concerning patients who go to the hospital from the emergency room, from the clinic, and those who come for elective service including same-day surgery not in critical situation.

In all the cases, respect and focus on the issue are of utmost importance to understand the situation and offer a solution with the participation of the patients.

The care for the sake of simplicity can be divided into office or/and hospital care.

Office Care

The key word here is "everybody involved."

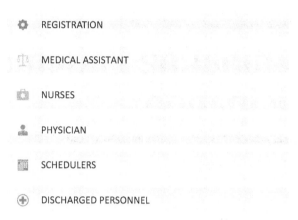

REGISTRATION

MEDICAL ASSISTANT

NURSES

PHYSICIAN

SCHEDULERS

DISCHARGED PERSONNEL

Hospital Care

The requirements for this care are as follows:

- Registration
- Lab techs
- X-ray techs
- Admission personnel
- Nurses
- Physicians in ER
- Nurses on the floor
- Healthcare personnel
- Physicians on the floor
- Social workers
- Case management
- Transporters.

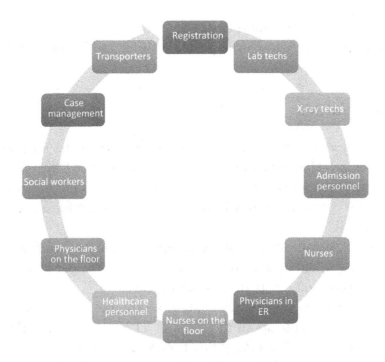

Assurance to Each Step of the Way

Many administrators describe "throughput" as the time interval between a patient's entry to the hospital and their discharge. But the same people forget that it is all linked to the flow of services required for the patients to go through the hospital without any bumps. Once the patients are discharged, that we all need to remember is the follow-up call. It is very important to note that the cycle of throughput will not be complete just after the discharge of patients.

The points that are essential in the patient flow are as follows:

1. The door-to-door process explained
2. Greetings when visiting hospital or clinic
3. Explanation of the process
4. Explanation of health insurance benefits

5. Referral explanation and help
6. Phone call follow-up after both clinic and hospital visits.

Core Values

Being patient-centered is the core value of medicine for many physicians. The principles of patient-centered medicine date back to the ancient Greek school of Cos. This school for the first time showed interest in the quality outcome for each patient [3].

Today, we apply a similar concept that can be described as the total person approach to patients' problems, particularly in the hospital setting "patient-centered care."

The physician should evaluate both the patients' disease and their thoughts about the disease. The impact of the diseases on the patient's daily functioning and their expectations of what should be assessed need to be investigated. The personal touch and explanation of the disease is also essential since it helps to understand the disease's progress and reaction from the patients.[1]

The next step is that the patient and the physician need to find a common ground regarding management. If there is no acute illness, the physician should engage the patients in prevention measures and health promotions. Creating a good patient–physician relationship is essential at this point in time. But the physician needs to be realistic about the success of the treatment and should communicate to the patient.

According to Stewart,[1] patient-centered encounters result in:

1. same duration of office visit (Epstein-frank [13])
2. better patient satisfaction (Epstein-peters [14])

---

[1] Stewart M, Brown JB, Donner A, McWhinney IR, Oates J, Weston WW, Jordan J. The impact of patient-centered care on outcomes. *J Fam Pract* 2000;49(9):796–804.

3. higher physician satisfaction (Epstein Fiscella [12])
4. fewer complaints against malpractice (Gerteis [6]).

How to Invite Patients to Participate?

The definition of healthcare and patient-centered care is keep changing; hence, the healthcare system has to adapt to it.

With social changes in medicine and evolution of the population, which now is covered by Medicaid, new patients, who have not seen a physician ever, come to the hospital. They represent an additional challenge.

First, we need to engage the patients, but it is challenging. Having insurance policy and consulting a doctor do not magically wipe years of bad habits away. Patients are accustomed to play a passive role in their care. Simply asking "do you have questions" will result in no answer and no questions.

A patient-centered approach should do more. The patients should be encouraged to participate more in the treatment plan to make them feel comfortable, so that they can interact more with the physician and get more understanding about their illness.

One of the best methods is the reverse question method in which the patients will be asked to explain what they understood and what they need to do.[2] By engaging patients in their own care, we can expect better results and definitely better adherence to the clinical plan.

Medicine is moving toward a more centered care approach, and we need to adopt even though we still do not know how to reward physicians who actively support this approach. The pathway is delineated because it seems to be the right thing to do.

---

[2] The Values and Value of Patient-Centered Care, *Ann Fam Med* March/April 2011;9(2):100–103.

Hudson et al. commented: *Because investments in improving patient-centered care are being undertaken on a large scale, developing adequate measures has taken on some urgency. How can we know whether interventions intended to enhance patient-centered care have achieved their goals? How can we meaningfully reward practitioners and health systems that complete patient-centered care? Patient-centered care is the right approach by engaging them and respect their preferences* [15].

Suggested Reading

1. Rogers C. *Client-Centered Therapy: Its Current Practice Implications and Theory.* Cambridge, MA: Riverside Press; 1951.
2. Neuman B, Young RJ. A model for teaching total person approach to patient problems. *Nursing Res* 1972;21:264–69.
3. Committee on Quality of Health Care in America. *Institute of Medicine. Crossing the Quality Chasm: A New Health System for the 21st Century.* Washington, DC: National Academy Press; 2001.
4. Rogers CR. The characteristics of a helping relationship. In: Rogers CR, ed. *On Becoming a Person: A Therapist's View of Psychotherapy.* Boston, MA: Houghton Mifflin; 1961;39–58.
5. McWhinney IR. Patient-centered and doctor-centered models of clinical decision making. In: Sheldon M, Brook J, Rector A, eds. *Decision Making in General Practice.* London: Stockton; 1985;31–46.
6. Gerteis M, Edgeman-Levitan S, Daley J, Delbanco T. *Through the Patient's Eyes: Understanding and Promoting Patient-Centered Care*, 1st edn. San Francisco, CA: Jossey-Bass; 1993.
7. Balint M. *The Doctor, his Patient, and the Illness.* New York, NY: International Universities Press; 1957.
8. Entralgo PL. *Doctor and Patient.* New York, NY: McGraw-Hill Book Company; 1969.
9. Guyatt G, Montori V, Devereaux PJ, Schünemann H, Bhandari M. Patients at the center: In our practice, and our use of language. *ACP J Club* 2004;140(1):A11–2.

10. McWhinney IR. An acquaintance with particulars.... *Fam Med* 1989;21(4):296–8.
11. Epstein RM, Street RL Jr. *Patient-Centered Communication in Cancer Care: Promoting Healing and Reducing Suffering.* Bethesda, MD: National Cancer Institute, NIH; 2007.
12. Epstein RM, Fiscella K, Lesser CS, Stange KC. Why the nation needs a policy push on patient-centered health care. *Health Aff (Millwood)* 2010;29(8):1489–95.
13. Epstein RM, Franks P, Shields CG, Meldrum SC, Miller KN, Campbell TL, Fiscella K. Measuring patient-centered communication in patient-physician consultations: Theoretical and practical issues. *Soc Sci Med* 2005;61(7):1516–28.
14. Epstein RM, Peters E. Beyond information: Exploring patients' preferences. *JAMA* 2009;302(2):195–7.
15. Hudon C, Fortin M, Haggerty JL, Lambert M, Poitras M-E. Measuring patient perceptions of patient-centered care: A systematic review of tools for family medicine. *Ann Fam Med* 2011;9(2):155–64.
16. Kinmonth AL, Woodcock A, Griffin S, Spiegal N, Campbell MJ. The diabetes care from diagnosis research team. A randomized controlled trial of patient-centered care of diabetes in general practice: Impact on current wellbeing and future disease risk. *BMJ* 1998;317(7167):1202–8.
17. Street RL Jr, Makoul G, Arora NK, Epstein RM. How does communication heal? Pathways linking clinician-patient communication to health outcomes. *Patient Educ Couns* 2009;74(3):295–301.
18. Arora NK, Weaver KE, Clayman ML, Oakley-Girvan I, Potosky AL. Physicians' decision-making style and psychosocial outcomes among cancer survivors. *Patient Educ Couns* 2009;77(3):404–12.

Chapter 12

Scheduling

Challenges

The scheduling processes followed currently do not take into consideration the needs of the patients and their families. The challenge lies in adopting a scheduling method that can help in decreasing waiting time. Another negative factor is that scheduling has no room for emergency or differentiation based on the severity of patients' problems. Every patient is treated as a warm body, and nobody knows what they really need until they visit the clinic. We cannot make the family understand the acuity both because they do not realize the severity of patient's condition and because we have an incomplete picture since they are not prepared to understand the process and system constraints of their local doctor's office and/or hospitals. This situation results in patients being angry, frustrated, and insulted when their concerns are not given immediate assessment and attention. Essentially, for a better scheduling design, we need a triage systems in which acuity and expectations are preset and the patients feel they are treated with dignity and respect. This can help also to decrease anxiety and fear.

Since the corporation took over healthcare, they have been trying to introduce programs for patients based on manufacturers' standards. Unfortunately, scheduling patients is not just scheduling their appointments. The patients are in a dynamic state; therefore, it is not a preset state but a state that can be changed and evolved.

We, therefore, introduce ad hoc scheduling and triage strategies, which permits preference to emergent patients, reallocation of patients, possibilities of cancellations, rescheduling, and last-minute appointments.

Bringing this method to practice would not only increase the clinical benefits but also reduce the number of visits to the emergency department (ED). Thus, a large number of patients would choose the ED to support their needs when they cannot get or wait for a clinic appointment. These needs should be taken care of in a clinic setting to decrease the load on hospitals and ED.

It is possible that a physician could be available for home visits as in Europe. This can help the patients having difficulty in mobilities due to lack of transportation be treated at home, and the need for ambulances or transportation will decrease.

Staff can be reallocated when emergent and acute visits are needed. The team and the clinic should be working in a dynamic state as well. On the contrary, most of the clinics have preset schedules and do not permit changes in scheduling and patient status, which is normal and typical in healthcare industry.

The model of ambulatory healthcare is based on intermittent visits to a physician's office, in either private practice, group practice, or hospital-based clinic. Many factors can constrain the access to appointments: system design, which includes geographic availability, hours of operation, IT capability, and practice management; availability of providers, which includes provider's expertise, number of individual preferences, and accountability; and the ability of patients, which includes their choice, transportation, and insurance status. The system is exploding and definitely will need a redesign, not at the national but the local level.

We think that the major issue is to try to apply a standard model all across the U.S., because each area of the country has different typology of patients with different needs and backgrounds, which should be considered when scheduling the patients.

In the acute care setting, Brandenburg reported that: ... *the traditional model of managing patient flow based on acuity alone resulted in significant wait times for patients with issues that were not life-threatening. As a result, new approaches have been developed, such as "fast track" treatment, to provide care for patients not requiring complex acute care, real-time visualization of wait times, and active bed management for hospital admission. Other methods such as decanting care to non-ED settings and predictions of patient demand have also been increasingly used methods to address the wait times.*

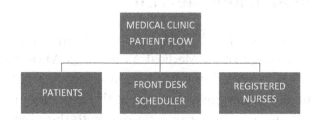

Patient Utilization Ratio

According to the patient engagement rules, physicians can help drive access to care for patients. Unfortunately as reported in the web,[1] ... *when patients do need to access in-person care, they often face complications with scheduling appointments. When contacting a provider's call center or front desk to make*

---

[1] https://patientengagementhit.com/features/what-providers-should-know-to-improve-patient-access-to-health care.

an appointment, patients may encounter busy signals, techno-logical issues, or troubles finding a time that meets both patient and provider needs.

The problems of a particular area in a country include the lack of the physicians, which is resolved by other healthcare providers such as nurse practitioners and physician assistants. The dissatisfaction of patients about the practice is now extending to those healthcare providers, who are already in the stress of working in certain areas, frustration with the job, and pressure from corporative healthcare organizations that are not prepared to run clinics efficiently, thus ruining the relationship with their providers. In the end, all of these affect the patients, their access to care, and the scheduling of their appointments, which is 4–8 weeks after their call for help.

More healthcare providers are needed, but better organizing skills and supportive healthcare cooperation to the providers are a must to provide better patient care.

Preparation before the Visit

It always works best for the patient to have some training and teaching by a nurse or an Medical Assistant (MA) or a support group before meeting with the physician. Not only does this save time but also give the patient the capability to focus and concentrate on a better one-on-one with the physician. The patient needs to know what the problem is and wants to know what can be done about it naturally and precisely. It is essential to concentrate on the issues, let the patient bring forth the problems, and answer all the questions.

Can technology help? For sure, electronic billing and electronic medical records can help. It is essential to reevaluate the vendor contract annually and write another contract. Review the telecommunication cost and your computer cost for the allocation of information. Scrutinize new insurance to check if it is worthwhile to go with new coverage under a new contract or is it better to stay with a deal that has been set up before. Treat well the staff as much as possible because those are your assets. Avoid long-term storage by using a better and simpler supply chain process (see Ref. [1]).

Payment Transparency

To help patients make their payments, specifically in case of high out-of-pocket costs, the healthcare organizations set up and offer payment plans, credit card payments, and so on to allow patients to pay in installments and decrease the "scare" of the big final bills from hospitals, procedures, and so on.

Even if it seems a visible action to create payments, easy installments have been successful in decreasing the worry of the financial issues of the patients, helping them to focus more on their medical needs.

We need a healthcare organization to create and practice price transparency. Even physicians do not have a direct answer when we ask about the price of a procedure and that affects the provider and the patients. The other issues are related to the ballooning price. We need to ask the organization to provide the patients details of the real cost and not the balloon price which they can claim from health insurances. The ballooning I purposely have done since the health insurance always cut 30%–50% of the reimbursement; this is a game in which patients should not be a victim and which needs to stop.

There is a demand—the patient needs something and a responsible physician or provider notices them and gives an answer and clinical plans. Providers have to ensure that patients receive treatment regardless of their circumstances.[2]

---

[2] Brandenburg L, Gabow P, Steele G, Toussaint J, Tyson BJ. 2015, Innovation and Best Practices in Health Care Scheduling, National Academy of Sciences, https://nam.edu/wp-content/uploads/2015/06/SchedulingBestPractices.pdf.

Suggested Reading

1. Frezza EE. *The Health Care Collapse.* New York: Routledge Publishing, 2018.

Chapter 13

Do Patients Want to Participate?

Lack of Ownership

Patients' lack of ownership in their health is the trademark of US healthcare. When people are sick, they go to the hospital; in the meantime, they do whatever they want, such as smoke, drink, and gain 200 lbs above the supposed healthy weight. This is a system that rescues patients! But you cannot be revived completely. If you are sick and if you have not taken care of yourself for years, maybe nothing can be done for you.

What has been lacking is having a plan and a strategy to teach the patients how to take care of themselves as much as possible. In the countries with social systems health care, patients do not go to the emergency room unless it is necessary; they have a physician on call, instead. They try to modify their diet and lifestyle, reduce smoking habits, and so on to be healthier.

Chronic diseases like diabetes, emphysema, arthritis secondary to obesity, and so on can be cured by better educating the patients.

More critical though, we need to work on the basics as well by training the new patients for a better and healthy life by making them more self-conscious, self-caring, and enhancing their understanding of what they have to do to achieve it, in addition to giving them the protocol and policies to sustain a better life.

Prevention has always been the pinnacle of any medical care. It should be brought back as the basement on which new healthcare for the next century can be built.

Revolution in Approach: Do Patients Want to Participate?

The medical field has depended on the trust placed by the patient on the physician to make the right decision. We defined this as a "paternalistic system" in our previous publication.[1] Nowadays, the pendulum is swinging; the patients no longer listen to their doctor's suggestions, and they want and need to participate in their treatment plan. Rather than simply ordering and advising, clinicians should have a conversation with the patient about the order and plans of treatments provided.

It is like a roundtable approach where the patients are informed and trust the physicians to suggest the right options.

During our younger days, patient–physician interaction was limited to only listening to the physician; today, we have both the talk and listen options. This means that patients can also ask questions, and they are encouraged to do so. Though most patients feel educated after having done their research on the web, we advise them against it since the Internet also has information written by nonexperts in the field. These nonexperts do not have the required background and knowledge to publish their video or their advice, thus creating problems and confusions in the process.

---

[1] *Medical Ethics*, book by Frezza EE.

Therefore, we need to encourage patients to be proactive about their health within the context of this provider–patient relationship, but we will continue to advise the patients to listen only to experts and not the "Monday-morning quarterbacks."

It will be fantastic to create and share documentation, have a shared decision-making process, and work on common goals and treatment that patients and families share and agree upon, similar to having a contract to purchase a house. Alerts and alarms about side effects should be written in a way that can be shared with the patient.

The problem that we face is that most of the patients do not prefer to take responsibility and "vomit" all the blame for their care on the physician. Most of the patients I have been in contact with do not want liabilities, and hence if something goes wrong, they blame or file lawsuits against physicians.

This is too easy because their health starts with them, and if they do not do anything to fix themselves, the physicians do not have magic wands.

Sharing views and decisions starts with compliant patients. For healthcare issues, we cannot blame only the physician, but also the lack of education and lack of penalties to the patient. Even though a patient does not follow their treatment plan or refuses to follow physician's suggestion, it becomes the physician's fault. This cannot happen when the patient is at home, because in home the patient is in charge of their own health. Some common sense in the patient population can also help a lot!

Patients Should Be Open to Criticism

If a physician welcomes the patient's feedback, the patient has to do the same, and not just post an ugly criticism about the physician on the web just because they can do so! It is not possible to have a shared vision with patients that cancel their visits at the last minute—the system fails. Such patients do not care that the time alloted to them in the clinic could be used for someone else who really needs to see the provider that day. They are not bothered about others as they do not even care about the physician. If they do not buy the medicines, get the appropriate workup, meet the radiologist, etc., they have no consequences whatsoever.

These situations place even more stress on the physician and require them to share their plans, which means that the patients need to be involved in every step. The physicians need to perform many tasks, but lack the counterpart, the patient, who will work with them. The physicians deserve a better partner in the form of professional patients, and not just patients. Those that don't want to be professionals should not seek advice that they will not follow through. Physicians have to face many consequences if they don't do their job correctly, but not the patients. The patient should also be held accountable for their mistakes, and their mistakes should be reported to their health insurance companies, based on which their claim would be approved or not.

If you book a room in a hotel and you do not stay, you lose the deposit, whereas the patient does not lose anything except their health. Patients need to be responsible for themselves and others since if they don't show up in the office, they take the place of somebody else who is waiting for that place. If they cancel a surgery the night before, they take precious time of another human being that might need the surgery more than them.

This reflects badly on the patients and shows a complete lack of care for themselves and the society they live in. Unfortunately, in today's healthcare, everybody is providing care to them, but no one wants to point out their mistakes, which is wrong since we are perpetuating a negative attitude and situation that may affect the life of another human being.

Professional Patients

If we want patient-centered care to work, we need to have patients to be professional as well and not be ignorant toward their health, skipping their scheduled labs and tests just because they "forgot." The forgetful patients need to be educated, and if their "forgetfulness" persists, they need to face the consequences and be fired both as the patient and as the member of their healthcare insurance because they become a liability not just to the system but overall for themselves.

We live in a democratic country—the patients can do whatever they want—but they cannot come back and blame others for their "forgetfulness." Let us stop this madness and get the health care back in shape.

We Need Happy Physicians

Too many people have forgotten that besides the patients, even the physicians and the providers are customers of healthcare; without them, healthcare will not exist.

If all the administrators are taken out of the hospital, it will still be a business as usual, but if you take out physicians and nurses, the hospital will close at the earliest.

Hence, it is about time we consider the physicians as valuable customers of our healthcare and not just a mere worker. The physicians need a reason as to why we wake up in the morning, and they do this job to help and provide healthcare to others. Patients deserve happy physicians.[2]

---

[2] Smith CW, Graedon T, Graedon J, Grohol J. May 16, 2013. In Society for Participation Medicine. A Model for the Future of Health Care.

Suggested Reading

1. Frezza EE. *The Health Care Collapse.* New York: Routledge; 2018.

THE TRUE NORTH

Chapter 14

Transparency and Honesty

Honesty with Patients

The relationship between the healthcare worker and the patient is grounded in more respect for trust and ethical principles.

The willingness of one party to be vulnerable to the action of another party as an expectation that the other will perform a reaction important to the trust is irrespective of the ability to monitor control over the other party, by definition the patient, is a disadvantage.

Convey things the way they are—sugar-coating will not help—don't hide information, and check old charts.

Consent

Patient autonomy strives toward equality in this partnership that changes a relatively new relationship; a significant change in law and medicine will change the relation. In the beginning, a simple consent was required for the treatment of a specifically invasive procedure.

The landmark was achieved in 1914 by Judge Benjamin Cardozo who stated that *"every human being of adult years and sound mind has a right to determine what shall be done with his own body; and a surgeon who performs an operation without his patient's consent commits an assault, for which he is liable in damages."* This was part of a verdict in New York Hospital.[1]

Following are the ethics background we need to follow:

■ Medicare, Medicaid, and Veterans Administration have placed an emphasis on the road justice and treatment of the patient since the public think that medicine has all kind of legal and ethical problems
■ Many nurses and physicians practice day by day ethics more than anybody else, probably in any profession
■ Honesty is, in essence, the act of transferring medicine fairness in all human interactions
■ Deception and lying are considered to be inherently wrong by most moral and religious traditions
■ The potential benefit of disclosing information outweighs the possible harmful consequences as they would increase emphasis on patient autonomy on equal partnership.

We need to keep in mind that:

■ the patient requires information to make a decision
■ in modern times, it is challenging to keep the truth away from the patient because there is a lot of web information and basic knowledge easily available
■ in Europe and Latin America, the family can ask not to release information so as to protect the patient from psychological events in case of terminal illness
■ this is something that needs to be discussed with the family with the power of attorney.

---

[1] www.olender.com/articles/informed-consent-every-patients-right/.

Welfare

Understanding the importance of morality is the most important outcome in any societies in the medical profession. Advocacy for patient interest and health requires the following competencies:

- Having a good practice
- Interpersonal skills
- Making the correct decisions
- Avoiding mistakes.

Global Trust

Global trust is difficult to achieve. It requires the following:

- Honesty, which tells the truth and avoids intentional false hope
- Confidentiality, which is a proper use of the sensitive information
- The global trust is the soul of faith or aspect that combines elements from some or all of the other dimensions.

Building Trust

The central theme of building trust is honesty and trustworthiness brought on a professional, organizational, and individual level. It involves the following:

- Understanding how human pain can be related to trust
- The initial development of faith is gained during the first meeting where all the issues need to be presented, including present problems, complications, and future treatment

■ Trust means that you continue to talk to the family to be sure that all understand the situation and share the same views
■ The initial confidence is based on global and professional respect
■ Several studies have shown that the deciding factor for trust in the physician is the interpersonal relation between the physician and the patient, which is usually established before the surgery
■ The same strategy applies to the nurse; the relationship has to be built in the first few hours of taking care of the patient
■ The physician and the nurse need to be present to explain any consent and translate it very well as required.

Patient Autonomy

The pendulum is swinging from the physician–healthcare worker decision toward absolute patient autonomy, and the emphasis on relationship and trust building is becoming more critical.

Errors

■ The error may not result in an adverse event but can still be troubling to the patient
■ The American Medical Society Association states that the physician should at all times deal honestly and openly with the patient
■ At the international level, there were a lot of initiatives in Australia and United Kingdom taken to decrease the medical errors by discussing with the patient
■ In the United States in 2005, at the same time the campaign was launched in Australia and United Kingdom, Senators Hillary Clinton and Barack Obama sponsored a bill—The National Medical Error Disclosing and Compensation Act.

Disclosure

- Disclosure would increase the likelihood of malpractice action
- This concern has done much to impede the flow of information to the patient and family
- Despite this, it is now clear that the patient wants to know about all the errors that cause them harm
- Another study showed that the patient would be less likely to seek legal advice when the error was disclosed
- The leader of hospital administration needs to be involved in revealing a process and offer emotional support to patient and family if required
- The patient should also be told what measures would be taken to assure that the scenario does not occur in the future to another patient.

Legal Aspects

The legal aspect of the medical profession that every physician and healthcare practitioner is concerned with to some degree is to avoid the involvement of a medical malpractice lawsuit.

Protecting the patient from harm is no doubt a primary concern at the foundation of every medical practice of any professional. The professional should include a plan to reduce both the risks by utilizing protocols standard. We need to develop standard care and best practice, and develop skills for effective patient–physician communication. This type of model can help reduce the number of medical errors or anticipated outcomes that occur and assist the physician to effectively manage this event.

There are a few things the healthcare providers can and cannot do to help the situations. They are described in the following.

Arrogance

- Arrogant, inattentive nurses and physicians are more likely to have a lawsuit filed against them, not necessarily because of the outcome of medical mix-up, but just because of the negative psychological impact they make on the patient
- Almost every medical malpractice case is secondary to unsatisfactory unanticipated consequences
- Most of them are based on the lack of sympathetic concern and respect.

The Power of Apology

One the most effective forms of communication is an apology, which need not be an admission of fault or negligence but should be a demonstration of compassion and understanding. "I'm sorry" may be a common phrase, but it needs to be phrased in a way that means it.

The physician's ability to accept the reality, recognize the responsibility, and remedy might always be visible when an apology is appropriate. An apology should not be reserved solely for the medical mix-up but is also necessary for situations of less severity, such as a long wait before an appointment, bad behavior by staff, delay in returning telephone calls, or delay in answering when the nurses call into the room.

Transparency and Outcomes

An overwhelming number of studies show that apologies and transparent disclosure are the best risk management tools.

- The standard requires healthcare organizations to disclose unanticipated outcomes of care or treatment for the patients

- When appropriate, their families should also be informed about issues of concern, including any unintended consequences
- A sense of compassion and understanding of the pain— after the apology—needs to be genuine
- An independent practitioner knows always how to explain the outcome of any treatment or procedure to the patient, and when appropriate, to the family
- Whenever those outcomes are significantly different from anticipated results, it can spark some controversies because not all adverse effects are caused by medical error or negligence
- The first step must be a collaborative effort with family and patients to structure the plan of action, which can help assure complete and timely disclosure of the event
- The standard does not require documentation of exposure, but to avoid any doubt, requires a team approach of having more than one witness to be present during the release of information
- The American Medical Association has had similar ethics requirements as part of their code of ethics, and its fundamental ethics require that the physician should, at all times, be honest and open to with the patient
- In situations where the patient suffers a significant medical complication, the physician is ethically required to convey all facts necessary to ensure the patient's understanding of what has happened
- Patients seeking medical care place themselves in a precarious condition. To entrust their life in the hand of somebody else is what the patient does by going to see a physician.

Therefore, the patients' understanding of what the procedure is and what their consequences are is of utmost importantance. The patients should have the amount of information required to make an informed healthcare decision.

Chapter 15

The True North Alignment

Improving Patient Relationships

If we have a compass, we look toward the true north to get direction. If we look closely, the only way to achieve the true north is to improve the relationship with our patients. There are no tricks or hidden agenda. It is simple and easy.

There are a few ways of improving patient-centered care in your hospital environment and ensuring the true north is reached.

1. Make sure staff members understand their roles
2. Set department-wide and hospital-wide goals
3. Reward the best performers
4. Set clear guidelines
5. Work closely with patient advocates.[1]

---

[1] www.gebauer.com/blog/5-ways-hospital-administrators-can-improve-patient-centered-care.

Align Patients and Physicians

One of the most challenging tasks in having good patient care is to align the different components:

1. Front desk staff
2. Phlebotomist
3. Support system (social service, nutritionist, respiratory therapist, physical therapists)
4. Medical assistants
5. Nurses
6. Physicians.

Without counting the other people involved in keeping the clinic and the hospital clean, supply chain always has to be up to date and ready to go.

Meetings should be arranged to set the goals for all. Separate meetings may be necessary to address each section's need.

It is instrumental in having billboards, in discussing issues with the staff and in the boardroom, to have a ready exam room and a clean break room.

Everybody needs to be aligned, from administration to the housekeeping.

What the Patient Expects

The patient expects clinical quality and dignity, and they need to feel important. Those two metrics should match both from the clinical survey and from the patient survey. As you understand, it will be instrumental in having an inquiry to both the staff and patients.

The loyalty of the patient depends on matching or exceeding their expectations. This is called patient experience, and this is what we aim at to keep the patient at ease and in the loop.

Building a team with your patient is always my suggestion to a physician—when they are part of the team and they understand the issues, they are more likely to participate and follow up on the directions.

True North

The true north is a concept made to inspire all of us to find and see the same north by turning the compass in the same direction, which means, the same answer, the same behavior, and the same better quality.

Together we inspire respect and kindness by serving as a trusted beacon of healing for all. To better understand that, we have made a graphic that summarizes the priority filter and our true goal or true north.

We are all human—the staff, the physician, and the patient—if we can act humanly among us, we can achieve the best results.

Human refers to patient/customer experience, whereas business refers to the clinical/business equation. The former will bring forth the human side of the patient, connecting the patient with you. This is the only way to have the patient on your side, which means that they will listen to you, they will share your vision, they will be comfortable, and they will be the best caretaker themselves while at home. This can help reach 100% compliance. Is that a good quality? It is the best quality.

It is therefore essential to explain what you are going to do, how long it will take, and why it is crucial to the patient or to the person.

We need to explain what we are doing and then ask if they have any questions. We need to tell what happens next, how long it will take, and then set the next goal for the therapy to be successful. This process is called "caring out loud."

It is important then to have "on-the-spot recognition" since it promotes awareness for the concepts and elements of the organization and it will encourage accountability for excellent patient and employee experiences.

Capturing positive stories are very essential to be used in future meetings, workshops, and practice publications.

It is also always good to have a person in the practice who can talk about their experience on a different disease and they can pass along their expertise to others.

A patient-to-patient experience sharing is one of the most successful methods for achieving 100% patient adherence.

What if we are short of or if we miss something? First, avoid blame that will create frictions. Make it an opportunity to learn and find new heroes for the next time. Follow your HEART:

1. Hear
2. Empathize
3. Apologize
4. Resolve
5. "Thank you" and track it.

You need to set your own culture to get a new culture. You cannot get the lifestyle you want just by desiring it. Make it happened; accountability is essential; if there are mistakes and lousy situations, take responsibility and solve them.

Graffiti

Negative Impressions

We call that graffiti! The following are usually the three most common reasons for the patients to not to visit the same provider again. In general, anything that detracts from subjective or patient experiences can be difficult to recover.

- A dirty office
- Verbal abuse
- Physical abuse.

How is everyone accountable for graffiti? The first thing is to be ready for a sincere apology; a fake one will not work. Make sure that you share the experience with your patient and be supportive; maybe you don't agree, but you can be supportive. It is crucial at that point to say the right things and do the right things. Protect your patient, and they will protect you.

Graffiti can be divided into physical and verbal. Graffiti can hurt the patient sensibility and your staff. Let's review them:

Physical Graffiti
- Trash in the visible area
- Food in the patient area or working station
- Clutter
- Broken furniture
- Broken equipment
- Crumpled taped and handwritten signs

- Staff's usage of cell phone or other phones in the patient-care area
- Negative body language
- Dirty clothes.

Verbal Graffiti

- It is not my job
- You are not my patient
- There is nothing I can do for you
- Inappropriate comments
- Inappropriate conversation
- Using difficult acronyms or words
- Gossip
- Negative comments about others
- Stereotyping people.

Chapter 16

Quality Values

Importance of Quality Values

Ronald Epstein wrote: *Patient-centered care has now made it to center stage in discussions of quality. Enshrined by the Institute of Medicine's "quality chasm" report as 1 of 6 key elements of high-quality care, health care institutions, health planners, congressional representatives, and hospital public relations departments now include the phrase in their lexicons. Insurance payments are increasingly linked to the provision of patient-centered care.*

Lost in many of the discussions of patient-centered care, however, is the essential and revolutionary meaning of what it means to be patient-centered. The originators of client-centered and patient-centered health care were well aware of the moral implications of their work.

The principles are simple:

1. Deep respect for patients as unique living beings
2. The obligation to care for patients on their terms
3. Patients are known as persons in the context of their social environment
4. Patients are respected and involved in their care, and their wishes are honored during their healthcare journey.

Unfortunately, it is difficult to have a focus at the same time on the patients' personal needs and also on the evidence-based approach, which tends to focus on scientific issues mostly.[1]

That debate has been put to rest: *"proponents of evidence-based medicine now regard what is meaningful and valuable to the individual patient more than anything else. Patient-centered care, as does evidence-based medicine, considers both the patient's needs and the science"*.[2]

Importance of Quality Personnel

Patient-centered care is matched to the quality of personal, professional, and organizational relationships. Thus, efforts to promote patient-centered care should be considered to measure patient-care quality.

The physicians, who were the leaders of the dialogues, are now trying to engage the patient and get active participation. Training is needed for physicians to be more mindful, informative, and empathic to transform their role and create, as Epstein wrote: *"a partnership, solidarity, empathy, and collaboration.systems changes that unburden primary care physicians from the drudgery of productivity-driven assembly-line medicine can diminish the cognitive overload and exhaustion that makes medical care anything but caring or patient-centered"* (Epstein).

Quality of the Doctors

The patient should be able to check the doctors' credential, their expertise, their fellowship and qualification, particularly

---

[1] www.annfammed.org/content/9/2/100.short.
[2] Epstein RM, Street RL Jr. The values and value of patient-centered care. *Ann Fam Med* 2011; 9(2):100–3.

now that information technology is widely used. The following should be built for patients to use:

1. Credentials on the web
2. Resume, background expertise on the internet
3. Flyer in the office with a picture and short bio.

Quality Medical Staff

If the doctor can research, this should be equal to the personnel. The nurses, medical assistants (MAs) specifically, need to have their web and bio available for the patients, including the years of experience and expertise in their everyday practices such as drawing blood, etc.

Proper Facilities

Both the hospital and the office need to have appropriate facilities built. Nothing is worse than going to a medical facility that is falling apart, smells bad, and has a lousy bathroom.

The facilities need to be easily accessible for everyone on foot, by wheelchairs, by ambulance, etc.

They need to have a comfortable and clean room in a way that the patient is relaxed and the physician can do a proper physical examination.

Understanding Insurance Benefits

Even if everybody thinks that it is the patient's job to understand their insurance benefits, what is paid by insurance, copayment, pay of the office, in the system or outside the system, most of the patients are clueless. These make the patients very nervous and on the defensive.

We must provide service to help understanding the benefits.

Understanding the office payment or cost of the procedure from the patient's point of view such that it is easy on the patient's pocket is essential and can improve the relationship with patients and their view of how they evaluate you or the office or the hospital. It has excellent quality value.

Good Follow-Up

Both the office and the hospital should have a follow-up phone call in place; personnel need to be assigned to follow-up with the patient understanding how they are doing. There need to be healthcare personnel with knowledge on medical issues and not just front desk personnel with no medical background.

Whoever is making the phone call also needs to be able to answer the patient's questions and issues.

Clear Instructions

One of the most common complaints from the patients is that they do not understand what they need to do when they get back home.

In the office, it is vital that your MA or a nurse will go again through the plan reviewed with the physician. In the hospital, it is imperative to have a nurse going to the room of the patients to do the "read back instructions."

It has been shown that adding a nurse to do that, as some hospitals think, will cost the hospital money without any gain from the corporation, but it makes indirect gains. By explaining the instruction one more time, the following things can be reduced or avoided:

- Phone calls
- Unnecessary visits to the office
- Unnecessary visits and return to the emergency room (ER)
- Return to the hospital.

All of these represent an extreme saving that will account for the indirect saving, and therefore, fewer expenses and fewer penalties by Medicare, but most of the time the hospitals forget that.

After Hours

Another thing the patient looks to evaluate a physician or an office or a hospital is the insertion of what to do after hours.

Who do they need to call? What is the number? When do they need to go to the ER?

Improving Clinical Outcomes

Person-centered approaches can improve clinical out-comes. Self-management support has been found to improve symptoms and findings in people with arthritis, asthma, diabetes, hypertension, heart disease, heart failure, stroke, cancer, and other conditions, at least in the short term.

There were better clinical outcomes when it was matched with improved adherence to medication.[3]

Core of Quality Measures

Peterson reported that *"Bases of provider quality mea-sures have been developed by accreditation organizations,*

---

[3] Why Person-Centered Care Is Important|Person-Centered Care..,
  personcentercare.health.org.uk.

regulators, payers, and healthcare providers themselves to measure specific areas of practice and performance. Indeed, several recent reports (by the Institute of Medicine and Bipartisan Policy Center, among others) addressing quality measurement have emphasized the burdens associated with reporting a large number of current measures and the sometimes inconsistent requirements for similar actions.[4]

A recent Kaiser Family Foundation/Commonwealth Fund survey found that *"half of the primary care physicians say the proliferation of quality measures to assess their performance has hurt the quality of care. The focused indicators that have been developed to assess the treatment of specific diseases or conditions are useful for encouraging the improvement of practice at the provider level. But, each is too narrow to tell us very much about how the health system overall influences the level of health in the population, even assuming that they were consistently reported and available to be analyzed (which they are not). Measures now used by payers – which often focus on health delivery processes believed to influence health and are typically used to compare quality across providers – may change over time as new quality improvement ideas come into vogue or older ideas get implemented by the vast majority of providers, which complicates their use as metrics for trends in quality over time."*[4]

Health Delivery

The changes in the healthcare delivery system and the nature of the medical profession have tempted physicians to abandon their commitment to their patients.

---

[4] Peterson. Measuring the Quality of Healthcare in the U.S. By Claxton G, Cox C, Gonzales S, Kamal R, Levitt L, Kaiser Family Foundation, www.healthsystemtracker.org/brief/measuring-the-quality-of-healthcare-in.

Health care today requires the interaction of many caregivers including the increasing government oversight, invasion of managed-care regulation, and more significant liability risk.

The cultural changes bring physicians to increased frustration due to a perceived loss of autonomy.

Non-constructive clinic behavior represents a persistent threat to patient safety and a response that affects others to carry out their duties efficiently, and that undermines the patient confidence in the healthcare team.

Physician adherence to core values of the medical profession is essential in creating a culture of professionalism and safety; this responsibility goes beyond the basic premise of the professionalism and is committed to the patient.

The behavior can directly impact patient safety in several ways. Initially experience of safe medication practices with intimidation evidence indicates that the nurses frequently do not protect patient–physician when necessary due to past abusive behavior.

The efficient system requires an ethical behavior, and as an actual component of the professional conduct, they also have been instrumental in introducing safety, self-regulation, and professional responsibility to establish and enforce the standard in most cases.

Suggested Reading

1. Crookshank FG. The theory of diagnosis. *Lancet* 1926;2:939.
2. Balint M. *The Doctor, his Patient, and the Illness.* London, England: Pitman Books Ltd; 1964.
3. Rogers C. *Client-Centered Therapy: Its Current Practice Implications and Theory.* Cambridge, MA: Riverside Press; 1951.
4. Neuman B, Young RJ. A model for teaching total person approach to patient problems. *Nursing Res* 1972;21:264–69.

Chapter 17

Optimized Healthcare Services

Individual Healthcare Needs

Reynolds and colleagues reported: *Patient-centered care focuses on the patient and the individual's particular health care needs. The goal of patient-centered health care is to empower patients to become active participants in their care. This requires health care providers to develop excellent communication skills and address patient needs effectively. Patient-centered care also requires that the health care provider become a patient advocate and strive to provide care that is not only effective but also safe. Patient-centered care is associated with a higher rate of patient satisfaction, adherence to suggested lifestyle changes and prescribed treatment, better outcomes, and more cost-effective care.*[1]

To make a comparison between health care and airlines, the patients judge the facilities in the healthcare services in the same way as they judge the comfort with airlines companies. They decide the quality based on how the

---

[1] Reynolds A. Patient-centered care. *Radiol Technol* 2009;81(2):133–47.

captain and the hostesses look in the same way they do with doctors, nurses, and other personnel. They assume the doctor is well trained, as they believe a captain has enough hours of experience to pilot an airplane. Criteria for judging a particular airline are personal and include aspects like comfort, friendly service, and on-time schedules. Similarly, patients judge the standard of their healthcare on nontechnical elements, such as practitioner's communication skills. They are not aware of the level of training and expertise of the practitioner.

Unfortunately, patients judge based on the manner the personnel behave rather than profound knowledge and technical abilities. The patients do not know. It is common that physicians with extensive experience and level of knowledge have less patience and assume the other should know a little, and they might lose patients even though they are the best doctor for the job.

Optimized Healthcare Services

If you ask anyone how to optimize the healthcare system, 90% of the people will suggest using technology. Computer system, web pages, and access to your information, and in general, an understanding of disease and plans by communicating with others through text and websites is the key that will take health care to the next level in the next century. Two of the next chapters are dedicated to these issues.

We are in a mixed system. There are a range of studies showing that person-centered approaches such as self-management support and shared decision-making can reduce service usage. For example, a Cochrane review of 36 self-management trials found that self-monitoring and agenda setting reduced hospitalizations, unscheduled visits to the doctor, and days off work or school for people with asthma. There is also evidence that when people are fully informed about the care and treatment, they choose less invasive and costly procedures.[2]

Besides that, the patient–physician personal relationship still is the *fulcrum* of all!! What can we do to optimize care then? Different concepts that are important for patients and physicians have been pointed out in the next sections.

For Patients

Online Charts

Access the web to check your data and learn about your problems and treatments.

Update Notes and Information

Opportunity to update your data is of utmost importance in patient-centered care that gives a chance to patients to participate.

Web Access to Doctors

Check what a doctor does and does not do; these specialties can help make a decision.

Email Doctors

Instead of hours spent on the phone, simple emails will do. It allows patients to focus on their questions and office than when answered in real time.

---

[2] http://personcentredcare.health.org.uk/person-centred-care/
overview-of-person-centred-care/why-person-centred-care-important.

Avoid Unnecessary Visits to the Emergency Department (ED)

With pre-answered questions, unnecessary time spent in the ED or the clinic can be avoided.

Optimize Admission

Schedule elective admission and optimize the patient optimize the patient before any surgery.

Improves Cost-Effectiveness

More communication results in fewer unnecessary admissions and drives the cost of health care down.

Better Patient Orientation

Patients can be better oriented as to what they should expect and the treatment, particularly by following respective web pages.

Understanding Co-Payments

Patients will better understand co-payment and out-of-pocket needs before they come to see a doctor.

For Physicians

Easy Referral to Other Physicians

This will help to communicate with another physician about your patients. It will make it easier if we can consult by web or email.

Optimize the Best Admission in the Best Hospitals

Not every hospital is the same; the services depend on their size and location. If patient information is received in advance, it will be possible in the future to send the patients for admission to the hospitals that has all the services required by them, thus avoiding unnecessary transport by ambulance or helicopter, saving the system lots of money.

Meet and Greet

The comfort experienced by the patients in the presence of a physician is the most significant impact on their experience. It is essential for the physician to make the people feel at ease. The following are some highly useful suggestions for the physician to get comfortable with the patients in the office as well as the hospital setting:

1. Greet them nicely
2. Sit down at the same level
3. Don't ask them to lie on the bed right away
4. Talk to them friendly
5. Get information informally
6. Perform the physical examination
7. Talk to them again
8. Answer to their questions
9. Greet and leave.

These form the basis for the interaction and also make the patients comfortable. Pain control is the next important question to address.

Performance Rate

Performance rate reflects the proportion of answers provided by clinicians for quality measures that indicate good clinical performance according to the measurement standards. Each answer given for a quality action is classified by Center for Medicare and Medicaid System (CMS) as "Performance Met" (good performance), "Performance Not Met" (poor performance), or "Performance Exclusion."

The UK Policies as an Example

In England, patient experience is one of the five domains of the National Helath System (NHS) Outcomes Framework, alongside which are evidence-based quality standards for patient experience in adult NHS services and service user experience in mental health. One of the six quality outcomes for the NHS in Scotland is that *"Everyone has a positive experience of healthcare." "**Individuals participating in their treatment and care:** Policy focuses on increasing opportunities and support for people to play a more active role in their health and health care, under the slogan 'Nothing about me, without me.' Specific national initiatives include shared decision making, care planning, and personal budgets."*[2]

The English Experience

A significant study was performed for the NHS in 2017,[3] and it found that "by *involving people in decisions about their health and care we will improve health and wellbeing, improve the quality of care and ensure people make informed use of available healthcare resources. Involving people in their health and*

---

[3] www.england.nhs.uk/shared-decision-making/about/
person-centred-care-and-shared-decision-making/.

care not only adds value to people's lives, but it also creates value for the taxpayer."[4]

The report from NHS continues and pointed out that *"Personalised care and support planning is a systematic way of ensuring that individuals living with one or more long term condition are supported through proactive conversations, with their clinician or health and care professionals. These conversations should focus on what matters most to that individual (their personal goals) and the support they need to manage their health and wellbeing. It should be a process of sharing information, identifying medical and non-medical support needs, discussing options, contingency planning, setting goals, documenting the discussion (often in the form of a care plan) and monitoring progress through regular review. People's lives can be transformed when they feel in control of their health and wellbeing and when they can shape their care, support and treatment to fit with what matters to them. When people are involved in decisions about their health and care (such as through personalized care and support planning or shared decision making), they tend to choose care, support or treatment packages that align with their personal preferences and goals. In other words, they make decisions and choices that help them optimize their physical and mental health and wellbeing."*

---

[4] From: Statutory Guidance for Clinical Commissioning Groups and NHS England, www.england.nhs.uk/wp-content/uploads/2017/04/ppp-involving-people-health-care-guidance.pdf.

Chapter 18

Healing Relationships

Biophysical, Social, and Spiritual Model

The biophysical, social, and spiritual model reveals that healthcare, which came from the patients-first philosophy, can be divided into four steps.

1. Biological: Genetic and pathophysiological mechanisms are explained in this area
2. Psychological: Develop and experiment with different factors within the mind of the person
3. Social: Cultural and environmental influences are the mainstream of this point
4. Spiritual: Assessment of individual spirituality and religion resources of each patient can help in their care.

All together, we need to find a peaceful balance between meditation, healthcare, the concept of spirituality, lifestyle, recreation, energy, fitness, etc.

Faith

Faith is regarded as an essential human force. A lot of people believe in something, and if it is not God, they believe in something else, but they still have a strong belief. A strong belief in something intangible or a potentially unproven feeling is most of the time described as faith.

Religion is something personal: something that you can change or improve. For sure, when patients are sick, faith comes stronger, and sometimes it can improve health profile, may reduce healthcare utilization, and at times make them better. It could also have a negative impact if the patients think they are being punished by the faith or the God that they believe in.

It has been shown that there is a connection between medicine and religion. The first people in the tribes that were administered medicine were the religious powers of the tribes themselves.

But there is also a large group of people that are atheists or agnostic who do not believe or think that religion is essential.

As a physician, we need to respect them all. We also need to understand that social situations can impact the spirituality and the beliefs of the patient because cultural or environmental influences are quite important in their religious preferences.

Assessment of the religions, resources, and preferences is critical when talking to the patient. In the past, most people have been known to claim that religion is fundamental in their life, and therefore, a lot of patients will welcome a physician inquiring about their spirituality.

Others prefer no spiritual source or prefer not even to talk about it. Others prefer an approach with a nonmedical therapy and a more comprehensive approach to their disease. Some others empower the body with spirits and health. There are four components that probably bring up the spirituality and the reaction of the patient toward their disease, namely, the body, the health, their spirit, and their mind—they are all interconnected. There are many ways to address spirituality.

There is limited knowledge and training about how to approach the faith and the spirituality of the patient.

Religions

The goals to widening your knowledge base about cultural and religious diversity are to reduce the incidence of poor patient outcomes, boost overall patient satisfaction, and improve care quality. This is applicable even while there are many other religious groups, as well as numerous sects within these groups and variations in belief within each faction, and can be specific to your patient population, which can optimize your patients' healthcare experience.

Belief or religion almost always plays some role during situations where the continuum of care has reached a point where discussion of end of life begins. Christianity, Judaism, and Islam all agree that the healthcare team should not impose life-sustaining therapies when the burden of treatment far exceeds the benefit or where such treatments will merely prolong the dying process. They support physicians' speaking openly about death and dying with the patients, being frank about the limits of medical care. They expect us to work hard to prolong life and never overtly take a breath, but recognize that there are limits when treatment should be withdrawn or withheld. There is no obligation to resort to every type of therapy in the effort to preserve life regardless of the likelihood of the outcome. Often, significant religions have some official statement about artificial nutrition and possible life-prolonging activities. Religion always defends human dignity.

Religion and Healthcare

Religion mostly expresses inner spiritual beliefs. Religion can be an organizing group of individuals, and there are more than 50 common religions that influence our culture.

A spirituality and religion survey in 2006 found that in the United States, 27% were Catholic and 7% Orthodox. At that time, the Islam religion was 2%, but this is much higher now. Protestants were 19%, other Christians 20%, Buddhists 5%, and spiritual people without having a defined religion were 19%.

A strong belief of something intangible was proven to make an impact in life.

Most people claim religion is fundamental in their life. Americans have a high prevalence of believing in God, 70% Christian, 5.9% non-Christian faith, 23% of religions are leisurely but are not affiliated. Seventy percent agree with physicians inquiring about spirituality, those who are not critically ill object, and those people with more faith are the ones that are critically ill and start believing in God because they feel sick or feel the need of supernatural help.

There is no question that body, health, spirit, and mind are intricate and are connected. Even in this area, the lack of a suitable environment plays a significant role. This is because sometimes the background is the primary and the most important thing that pushes people to spirituality or take some decisions.

Sometimes the lack of financial incentives or the lack of job makes people more focused on their real problems in life, and they don't have the time for religion. Eighty percent of the physicians believe they are obliged to present all options to their patients. Seventy-one percent can actually being referred to other physician in case procedure or more specialists visits are needed and the physician are in disagreement.

Per the American Medical Association, it might be ethically permissible for physicians to decline a potential patient when a specific treatment does not comply with the physicians' religious and moral beliefs.

Religious Coping

Religious coping has some positive aspects. Believing in one's love and care for the higher power can benefit the psychological recovery of the patient.

Meditation is now being used more in the Western world, while it was a common practice in the Eastern world.

How many times do we hear about the Eastern religion such as Buddhists and others spending hours and days or even years meditating in locations far away from the society and healing their body and the spirit?

Transcendental Meditation

Transcendental meditation (TM) is another type of meditation that was started in 1957 by Maharishi Mahesh Yogi. This meditation is practiced for 15–20 min twice a day. This is practiced by sitting comfortably with the eyes closed, being silent, with mental repetitions of simple sounds or mantra. This allows being quieter until the subconscious is healed. This helps bring peaceful thoughts and therefore relaxes your mind.

There were some tests and research performed on the physical reaction to TM. It is interesting to note that in some patients that were studied after TM, there was a reduction in metabolic activity, an increase in cerebral blood flow, skin resistant changes, and a decrease in plasma cortisol. How this is effective: Reduction in metabolic activity means that the body is calm and the stress is relieved; therefore, the body doesn't have to fight and produce hormones or antibodies or white blood cells. It has been shown, for instance, that in a situation of stress (article in *Lancet*), the amygdala can increase the production of white blood cells by strengthening the immune system. This weakens the body and hinders the treatment of cardiovascular disease, which can drive to heart attack and stroke.

Therefore, a reduction in metabolic activity is one of the mainstays in the treatment of stress and the treatment of the body. This relates to the action of plasma cortisol that can increase the tension by increasing other hormones, the fight or flight hormones, produced in the adrenal gland. This also increases the metabolic demand with an increase in sugar and high blood pressure. The same patient can develop type II diabetes secondary to the "burn of insulin."

The cerebral flow is increased in stress. Magnetic resonance imaging showed that compared to a baseline individual, the blood flow is decreased in patients after meditation, specifically in the parietal lobe.

Prospects

The spirituality brought to the arena of medicine is still a difficult subject to deal with for most of the physicians. Awareness about our religions and spiritual resources can improve the outcomes if there is a communication between the physician and the patient. Sometimes, just listening to the patient is sufficient. Decreasing the stress, being able to meditate, and being ready to take the time to pray, which can, in turn, be similar to meditation, could have a positive impact on the incidents of certain cardiovascular diseases.

Chapter 19

Information Power

A Technological Revolution

Patient-centered care is also sustained by the power of information. The patients now have the power to instantly access health information through their computers or mobile phones. Therefore, patients are better informed and are more active participants in their care.

Healthcare modernization has evolved and has been changing the way we practice medicine in the last 30 years. The need for improvement was the driving force behind the evolution of computers in healthcare. The majority of the past 30 years of technological expansion was spent on computer programs for administrative purposes, while the past decade has seen an emphasis on the clinical process.[1] Patient care has become a primary focus in the development of new concepts and knowledge in healthcare technology. Technological progress in clinical applications is the current trend in healthcare, and it will continue to play a significant role for years to come.

---

[1] www.himss.org/right-balance-technology-and-patient-care.

Best Outcomes Strategy

In response to the shift toward patient-centered care, the Biomedical Research Institute recently established the Patient-Centered Comparative Effectiveness Research Center (PERC).

As Solomon related to this problem, *Patient-centered outcomes research, also known as "comparative effectiveness research," focuses on identifying which of the existing treatment options will work best for patients. Studying the effectiveness of these treatment options (medical devices, surgeries, medications, etc.), researchers can determine which may most benefit patients and which may pose the most risk. ....researchers hope patients, caregivers, and their physicians will have the necessary information to make better-informed health care decisions that take into account patient preferences.*[2]

Knowledge Is Power

In interviews, patients expressed their worries that they were not completely informed about their condition or prognosis. To counter this fear, hospitals can focus on four kinds of communication:

1. Information on clinical status, progress, and prognosis
2. Information on processes of care
3. Information to facilitate autonomy
4. Health promotion.

Information Is Power

This concept is true everywhere including in medicine and healthcare. With the expansion of technology, obtaining the data is much easier than ever.

---

[2] Solomon DH, https://brighamhealthhub.org/treatment/what-patient-centered-care-means-for-you.

How many times in the ordinary conversations have you heard people say: "I don't know the issues, but I can Google it"?

It is becoming a standard. I have to admit that when talking to the patient, I often suggest them to Google the information I gave them and double-check.

It seems that if you give the patient a chance to research and double-check, you make them very comfortable and they are more likely to work with you.

Unfortunately, even with all the technology, most of the web pages do not carry the appropriate information; many YouTube videos are deviant and confusing. Hence, I always suggest that the patient check web pages from medical societies and not any outside the respectable medical sources.

How can information help the patient and the physician? Here is how.

For Patients

Gives Power to Patient

The patient feels more powerful if they can check the staff themselves. There is a sense of achievement and confidence that comes from that.

At Your Fingertips

How wonderful would it be for the patient to access a private web page from their office and check their X-ray, EKG, labs report, etc. in real time.

Make an Appointment

It can be very frustrating calling an office and waiting hours on the phone, when you can go on the web and make or cancel your appointment, choose your doctor, check out the doctor's details, and make the initial decision on your care.

Understand your Disease

On the office or the hospital web page, it is imperative for the patient to know how to read and be educated about their illnesses. This hospital web page should have more information that is educative and less on marketing. Patient needs to be informed and they need to feel comfortable, nothing else comes first; they do not need marketing when are in needs.

Talk/Text a Doctor

A few healthcare systems have been adopting the texting system for communications from a patient to a doctor. There are nurses assigned to it. This is an invaluable tool, particularly for senior people and for those living in a rural area.

Not only can you text but for a minimal fee, you can also talk to a doctor.

The same system has a doctor available to talk to you over the phone or the web for a fee comparable to an office visit.

Skype a Doctor

Telemedicine is becoming the innovation that will take over in the future. Do you want to drive or do you want to have your visit right from your living room? Well, we know the answer.

For Physician

Clarity of Plan of Action

There is nothing worse than not being able to understand what is going on with your patient because you cannot access other physician or hospital notes. What procedures have they had? What did the echocardiogram show?

Or better than having a very poor fax from other people's office and then finding out that the fax is missing a few pages.

Clarity of the notes, clarity of the tests done, and transparency on other people's plans of action are necessary and can be achieved only through sharing the system.

Unfortunately, there seem to be many systems on the market and they do not talk to each other. What is the point of pushing toward technology if the technology has a barrier? Mostly this is a business barrier—one company does not want to speak to the other company's system; the government should take the lead and allow all of them to talk.

It seems like a judge or a teacher telling the children what to do and how to go along. That is the present situation, which hopefully will improve.

Ability of Retrospective Analysis

With an electronic record, we can check many recordings of the patient from the past to clarify the present needs in a better fashion.

No Missing Paper or Labeling

How many times do you get labs and they forget to fax the last or the first page, and how many times is it the page that you really want to see? Well, the computer will have it all, no need for extra pages.

Communicate with Another Provider

A good system will allow the physician to communicate on a secure web about the patient and goals.

It will be a dream to be able to simply send a secure text to your referral doctors. It will be great if the other doctors can see your medical notes in real time.

It will save a lot of time and effort to ask a question to a cardiologist, to check if your patient is ready for surgery, and so on.

For the Healthcare System

Drive Physician to Do a Proper History and Physical

The electronic medical record (EMR) has forms that a physician has to click and fill. This makes it easy to write the information from the patients and to give an accurate picture without forgetting an essential part of the history and physical.

Drive Physician to Ask Appropriate Questions

If you forget to ask some information when you sit at the computer and you realize the part you are missing, you can always get more info and complete the empty spots and fill up all the information needed.

Show Physician the Missing Puzzle

Trauma, psychiatric history, neurologic history, and cardiac history can be a puzzle. By having a pre-printed form, all the mystery is already solved; you need to fill information, and the rest will be put together. Even medication dosage is calculated by the healthcare computer program in such a way that it always gives the appropriate dosages.

Help Connect Dots with the System

In theory, the electronic medical record should connect. In reality, they all come from different companies that encrypt the information in a way another system cannot access. This defeats the purpose of the electronic sharing of innovations.

Online Experiences

When patients find you online, as many do, either by accident or necessity, their first impression is your website.[3] Ensure real prescheduling expertise by:

- ensuring potential patients and current patients are able to tell exactly how to contact you in the first 3–5 s of visiting your website
- keeping your website free from potentially annoying distractions, like auto-starting videos, music, and flash elements
- being sure your website gives clear instructions on performing tasks such as filling out forms, scheduling an appointment online or via phone, contacting the office, finding you on social media, the location of relevant information, etc.

---

[3] www.beckershospitalreview.com/hospital-physician-relationships/patient-care-tips-to-ensure-a-positive-patient-experience.html.

Chapter 20

The Role of Technology and Telemedicine

Medical Devices

Patient care was highly complicated before the application of technology. Physicians relied heavily on their senses of sight, touch, smell, and hearing to monitor their patients. Over time, technology designed tools to detect physical changes in patient's conditions.

The technology adds other duties from the hospital. According to the Safe Medical Devices Act of 1990, which became effective in 1991, it *required* that healthcare facilities submit a report to the manufacturer and the Food and Drug Administration (FDA), comprising all incidents that reasonably suggest that the medical device might have contributed to a death or a severe injury or illness. Healthcare providers should be familiar with internal systems of reporting, as well as the FDA medical device reporting system.[1]

The FDA receives information about adverse effects related to medical devices from manufacturers, importers, and user

---

[1] www.fda.gov/safety/medwatch-fda-safety-information-and-adverse-event-reporting-program/reporting-serious-problems-fda.

facilities, so any problems with the device can be detected and corrected. Emergency Care Research Institute (ECRI) encourages the reporting of device-related incidents and deficiencies to rule out harm to patients.[2] Healthcare failure mode and effect analysis and sociotechnical proactive risk modeling offer methods for identifying equipment failures before they happen and strategies for preventing them.

Proponents of proactive risk modeling methods, relatively new to healthcare, suggest that physician and in general provider could play an active role in preventing equipment and technology failures and in responding appropriately to them should they occur.[3]

Keeping a Healthy Relationship

Registrations

The people working at the front desk do not realize their importance. They are the ones establishing the first contact and relationship with the patients, which is a critical factor for the success of a practice or a hospital.[4] Courtesy and friendship over the phone can go a long way.

Therefore, we need to set up more training for them to know how to talk to patients and not scare them off.

Relationship through Technology

Keeping a healthy relationship is the basis of patient-centered care. Electronic medical records are making it easier for

---

[2] ECRI's, www.ecri.org/PatientSafety/ReportAProblem/Pages/default.aspx.

[3] Nelson AL, Patterson ES. Patient Care Technology and Safety Gail Powell-Cope, www.ncbi.nlm.nih.gov/books/NBK2686/.

[4] www.beckershospitalreview.com/hospital-physician-relationships/patient-care-tips-to-ensure-a-positive-patient-experience.html.

patients to look up their findings and should be taken advantage of.[5]

An office with good instruments can impress the patients. How many times have you heard people talking about the optometrist or the dentist? Not really about the providers, but their new machinery in the office?

Nowadays, the technologies can help providers to enhance patient safety using real-time data such as blood pressure and respiratory rate. Having portable computer helps clinician to be more efficient.[6]

Technology is a critical factor defining the customer experience. It might enable interactions that improve responsiveness, account management, transition points, service delivery, pricing transparency, care readiness, staff utilization, and organizational flexibility. Despite all, the quality of the time spent between the physician and the patient is the basis of all healthcare and always will be.

Nelson reported: *Organizations are now being challenged to seek out solutions that enable them to create a brand associated with a premium customer experience. Digital tools and advanced technology provide a platform on which to increase that satisfaction, but it is essential to maintain a high-touch, high-quality, and highly interactive experience for all customers – not only for the patient, but also for the caregivers, clinicians, and other employees involved in the interaction.*[7]

---

[5] Civarro J, https://opmed.doximity.com/articles/how-to-create-a-positive-patient-experience-98f1bf1a9934.

[6] Zeise P. The Role of Technology and Patients in Patient Safety, www.healthitoutcomes.com/doc/the-role-of-technology-and-patients-in-patient-safety-0001.

[7] Nelson J, Principal, Deloitte Consulting LLP. The Role of Technology in the Patient Experience, https://blogs.deloitte.com/centerforhealthsolutions/role-technology-patient-experience/.

Healthcare Information

A vital element of healthcare information is documentation. We all have benefitted from these new concepts and continue to find more modern and better methods to improve patient care. *The electronic patient record has become an essential aspect of the information workflow which will result in better patient outcome quality and efficiency. Proper documentation is a vital skill in communicating the patient's condition and organizing their care according to the patient's needs.*[8]

Patient Education

Technology is beneficial in educating patients. The use of televisions, iPads, and other electronic devices by patients to learn and explore their illnesses and care is now the norm. Partnership with team members and families is essential for optimal treatment. Traditional patient education relied on written material about disease processes, medication, medical management, and self-care instruction guidelines.

Today, patients benefit from many computerized programs that enable them to understand the disease process and make important decisions about their health. Education improves patient self-care, satisfaction, moral support, coping skills, mental stability, patient security, and safety.

The power of information has multiple benefits, such as the following:

■ Reducing healthcare costs
■ Predicting epidemics
■ Avoiding preventable deaths
■ Improving the quality of life

---

[8] The Right Balance –Technology and Patient Care, www.himss.org/right-balance-technology-and-patient-care.

- Reducing healthcare wastage
- Improving efficiency and quality of care
- Developing new drugs and treatments.

With the shift to the electronic health record (EHR), healthcare facilities need to have expandable, cost-effective, and safe storage solutions. This is where the concept of Cloud comes in.

Telemedicine

Wikipedia describes telemedicine as the *use of telecommunication and information technology to provide clinical health care from a distance. It helps eliminate distance barriers and can improve access to medical services that would often not be consistently available in distant rural communities.*[9]

Telemedicine is the use of medical information exchanged from one site to another via electronic communications to improve a patient's clinical health status. Telemedicine can use different services: two-way video, e-mail, smartphones, wireless tools, and other forms of telecommunication technology.[10]

Starting over 40 years ago, with demonstrations of hospitals extending care to patients in remote areas, the use of telemedicine has spread rapidly and is now becoming integrated into the ongoing operations of hospitals, specialty departments, home health agencies, private physician offices, and consumer's homes and workplaces.[11]

Telemedicine can be used to refer to two-way video consultations or the transmission of healthcare data like electrocardiograms. Telemedicine can be of utmost importance in the fields of intensive cardiac, neuro, and critical care units in hospitals in rural areas that lack these specialties.

---

[9] Telemedicine - Sheridan Benefits, https://sheridanbenefits.com/why-choose-us/.
[10] Telemedicine – Mdstaffers, http://mdstaffers.com/services-2/telemedicine.
[11] Influences of Health Care Research Telemedicine – Running, www.coursehero.com/file/14807000/Influences-of-Health-Care-Research-Telemedicine.

Telemedicine requires a significant investment by hospitals and offices by buying new systems and improved internet delivery. Monitors, computers, and team training are needed to start a program.

There is no different in the reimbursement fee structure between services provided on site and those offered through telemedicine. American Technology Association (ATA) has historically considered telemedicine and telehealth to be inter-changeable terms.

Patient consultations via video conferencing, transmission of still images, e-health including patient portals, remote monitoring of vital signs, continuing medical education, and more are all considered part of telemedicine and telehealth.

What Are the Benefits of Telemedicine?

- Shorter waiting times for patients
  - Less crowded waiting rooms
- Improved access for rural areas
- Improved efficiency leading to savings.[12]

How Can Technology Help Health Care?

For this part, we have information from Christine Queally, who reported that *Communication failures are one of the most common factors that contribute to the occurrence of adverse events. EHRs are designed to help reduce those errors by compiling and maintaining all of the patient's health information into one easily accessible record. Prescribing errors are another common medical error that can potentially lead to severe complications. Electronic prescribing can help reduce prescription errors by allowing clinicians to send prescriptions electronically*

---

[12] Banova B. April 2018. The Impact of Technology on Healthcare, www.aimsedu-cation.edu/blog/the-impact-of-technology-on-healthcare/.

to the pharmacy. Medical alerts, clinical flags, and reminders are also ways technology can help reduce medication errors and improve patient safety. Information technology has drastically improved access to reference information. A broad range of drug-reference information is now available for hand-held devices, and clinicians can quickly access textbooks, databases, and other medical references online. It is fostering communication between providers and patients via online portals, text messaging, and email. It also increases access to information such as online medical records, which can improve self-monitoring and patient convenience — substantial impact on patient safety. As with most technology, there may be benefits and potential concerns. With any implementation or use of healthcare technology, it is critical to patient safety, and quality always remains the primary focus.

Christine Queally Foisey is the President & CEO of MedSafe.[13]

LONG-TERM AND CHRONIC CARE

Chapter 21

Continuity of Patient Care and Advance Directives

Patients express concern about their ability to care for themselves after being discharged from the hospital. The requirements for meeting patient needs in this area are depicted below.

 Detailed information regarding medications

 Physical limitations

 Dietary needs

 Coordinate and plan ongoing treatment and services after discharge

 Provide information regarding access to clinical, social, physical, and financial support continuingly.

There is a lot of work after the patient goes home; the care is not over.

We need to continue to deal with the issues and see how the patient recovers.

Hospital Discharge

This is the time to make all the appropriate connections. Social workers or case managers are required to build a relationship to set up home healthcare facilities, transfer, etc.

Send to a primary care physician (PCP) or assign a PCP if the patient does not have one.

Set follow-up expectations and book a follow-up appointment.

Prescription

For those who are not familiar with it, Meaningful Use is a government model that requires hospitals to implement certain transitions to electronic operating systems.

When the implementations are completed and the hospital can demonstrate a certain level of utilization, the government will make payments to the hospital to "reimburse" the cost of implementation. Meaningful Use includes an electronic record system and other items such as patient access portals and electronic prescribing. A certain percentage of prescriptions must be automatic to meet the metric. If the parameter is not met, the hospital may not get that reimbursement.

However, there are some challenges with e-prescribing:

- The nursing staff must obtain the patient's pharmacy info and enter it into the system
- Some pharmacies are not open at night
- Prescriptions sent electronically to a pharmacy that is not open may not go through or may not be available until the next day.

If the patient needs a prescription filled after hours, one can still e-prescribe it to the 24-h pharmacy.

Follow-Up Phone Calls

It is important to find out how the patient is doing and how they are feeling after discharge from the hospital or office visit. It is highly suggested to have one nurse in the hospital or in the clinic to follow up with the patient's conditions after the discharge. It will make the patient feel important, and they will be willing to comply with the hospital instructions.

After a clinic visit, the select patient should be followed up as well—those with needed clearance, new visit, specialties visit, and pre-hospital approach to the procedures scheduled.

Any patient doubted for poor compliance should be followed up routinely.

Critical Continuum of Care

Continuum of care implies the consideration of results providing ongoing care in situations where the outcome is becoming less and less predictable as to a defined end-point and most likely indicates the end of life. The physician in this ethical situation more than likely will be dealing not with the patient but with family and friends. The physicians will find themselves interpreting living wills and advanced directives. A legal guardian or appropriate next of kin will most often be a person with whom discussions occur.

Natural Death

Natural death applies a conceptual domain that encompasses "natural events." It excludes human participation and an unintended death. Many states now have added specific descriptions as a refinement to the patient self-determination act. Each state expects the physician to understand laws, be aware of their patient's wishes, and know who can act as spokesperson for the patient if they are unable or incapable of communicating their desires.

At the end-of-life scenarios, all the physicians walk a thin line.

Advance Directive

A mentally competent person will write advance directives or a living will that gives them the right to accept or refuse treatment without any explanation but does not allow steps to end life. Many patients when asked do not wish to be maintained on life support, but very few (less than 15%) have taken advantage of living wills.

Advanced directives or the living will infer the continuation of the necessities of life such as food, water, and air, but withdrawal or withholding of extraordinary support such as increased oxygen, antibiotics, and blood supporting medications is the focus.

There are several important points about current trends in our medical environment. In the United States, more than half of the patients treated via advance cardiac life support (ACLS) protocols in the intensive care units (ICUs) do not survive. Additionally, almost two-thirds of all Do Not Resuscitate (DNR) orders are written either after the first arrest episode or within 24 h of the first arrest. Although all possibly appropriate, from a time sequence, one cannot help but assume that for a number of these patients, no family discussions had occurred as to the real severity of illness/injury, with a potential DNR order being written well outside or before any risky procedure.

Life Support and Advance Directives

When patients are asked about their attitude toward life support, most (>80%) do not wish to have life artificially sustained. Yet when asked, very few (less than 10%) have had any discussion with their physician. Most importantly, of those who have had these types of conversations with their doctor, many patients had to initiate the debate! These statistics become even more alarming as we realize that up to 65% of deaths in the United States occur in ICUs.

Older patients with this situation may create a more straightforward process of decision-making. For these patients, the burden of treatment may easily or quickly exceed the benefits. The physician must not fore into applying life-sustaining therapy on persons for whom treatment will merely prolong the dying process. Possibly an 85-year-old might have an advanced directive; most likely, a 19-year-old does not.

The point at which the iatrogenic and disease-related discomforts of ongoing clinical care outweigh the clinical benefits for the patient, it becomes considerable to withhold or withdraw medical intervention and permit the disease process to complete its course. For a given patient, there is no set algorithm to say for sure when death will occur in the ICU.

Discussions of ethical nature, especially when dealing with the continuance of care or withdrawal of care, should have a set environment—a quiet place with few to no interruptions. The physician must sit at the eye level and should try to have support for the person making decisions in the form of one or two individuals with which they feel comfortable (ministers, close friends, or members of the family). The physician should set the stage for a discussion with appropriate opening remarks. Silence and listening are essential adjuncts to use—it helps those representing the patient to digest the information.

It is also crucial for the physician to instill hope, not that a cure is possible, but that the healthcare team will not abandon them.

Doctors' Fiduciary Relationship

We must remember that a doctor's relationship with their patient is fiduciary, that is, we are to serve the patients' best interest over our own. Once a physician determines that care is pointless, their decisions may involve withdrawal or withholding therapy. The discussion surrounding such decisions must stress that there is no set right or wrong way to alter care at the end of life. The clinical findings must be documented and discussed in understandable lay terms. They should be communicated as to how the family and friends should interact with the patient, encourage touching, talking, etc. There should be discussion as to what treatment and devices will be removed and what treatment will not be started.

ICU patients are unconscious, sedated, and often ventilated, so the end-of-life discussions taken by the family acting as surrogate decision-makers. These individuals must be made to understand that they are making decisions as the patient would have made if they were able to do so. This helps relieve guilt, especially when dealing with the withdrawal of care. Remind them that they are acting for the patient and must make decisions keeping what the patient would want in mind. Multisystem organ failure statistics predict a 20%–30% mortality associated to each vital organ; for example, for four organs' failure, there is almost 90% mortality.

Withdrawal of Care

What should be withdrawn or withheld? Ethically there is no difference between withdrawing and withholding cares. However, physicians and other members of the healthcare team tend to be more comfortable with withholding therapy than with withdrawing treatment.

Four elements that surround or describe a double effect are the following:

1. The act itself must not be intrinsically wrong. The intent is to relieve suffering, not to cause death, even though the process or therapy may hasten death
2. Intention: the person performing the effect must intend a good result
3. There must be a distinction between means and influence—good effect must be created directly. An unfortunate result cannot be a means to a good result. In other words, pain medication cannot be used to hasten death so that suffering or discomfort ends
4. Finally, the proportionality between good and bad effects must exist—the excellent outcome is sufficiently desirable to compensate for or allow for the adverse influence.

Ethics

We must monitor four principles as we approach these difficult situations:

1. Respect the capacity and autonomy of the individual to make their own decisions and choices
2. Do not harm (nonmaleficence)
3. Prevent and treat pain and suffering
4. Act reasonably and resolve dilemmas.

The secret to the care of a patient is caring for that patient.

It is no longer appropriate for the physician to be the patient's decision-maker. We must present medical facts that help the patient and their families should be informed. We can make recommendations, but it is the patient's decision.

There must be a collaboration with patients and families. Early on, after an illness or injury, the discussion should be initiated as to the goals and wishes of the patient, with specific emphasis on preference for life-sustaining measures. We must remember to provide information in lay terms as well as elicit and invite questions. We must ensure consistency between discussions and provide recommendations based on medically achieved goals. There must be open discourse about disagreements, and all should be done before the death is imminent.

Any time a physician finds themselves at odds with the family that cannot be solved quickly and easily, then the bioethics committee should be urgently consulted. Everybody should be allowed a gentle, peaceful death and respect for their dignity.

Suggested Reading

1. Frezza EE. *Professionalism and Ethics in a Surgical Practice.* Norwalk, CT: CineMed Publishing, 2008. (Covers two of the six requirements for the American Board of Surgery training competence.)
2. Frezza EE. *Principle of Medical Ethics.* New York: Routledge Publishing, 2018.

Chapter 22

Involvement of Family Members and Caregivers

When you finish talking to the patient, always ask them about their family and friends. Always ask them if they would like to involve other people in their care. If the answer is affirmative, get the consent from them to avoid a Health Insurance Portability and Accountability Act (HIPPA) violation.

Share Plans

If all clear, get the family in the room or the office and share the plan.

Sit down, or if in the office, move to a meeting room where everyone is comfortable and then review your assessment and plan. Make sure you ask the patient what you can share.

It is illegal to hide conditions such as the sexually transmitted disease. Hence, the law requires the physician to reveal this condition. In case of other diseases, the physician cannot disclose to the others without the patient's consent.

Support System

Who to call?

When to call?

Alternate and Surrogate

Healthcare Consent Act

Section 10 of the Healthcare Consent Act (HCCA) makes it clear that *The health practitioner proposing the treatment must decide whether the patient is mentally capable of consenting to the particular treatment recommended. If the health practitioner wants to get a second opinion, it is open to him or her to do so, but this is not a requirement before treatment is administered to the person. The health practitioner is deemed to be the "expert" in determining capacity as defined by the HCCA concerning treatment within his or her area of practice and expertise* [1,2].

Health practitioners can help to assess this situation except in those circumstances where the legislation requires that a "capacity assessor does the assessment."

These "capacity assessors" in the legislation are *the persons acting as assessors as so defined are required to perform capacity assessments by the "Guidelines for Conducting Assessments of Capacity" established by the Attorney General and dated June 7, 1996.*

Judith Wahl mentioned: *A person of advanced age or persons with physical or mental disabilities may still be capable of making all or some decisions for themselves. The definition of capacity does not make exceptions for age, physical disability, or mental disability. The key is whether the person understands the information that is relevant to making a decision and can appreciate the reasonably foreseeable consequences of the judgment or lack of the decision.*

Ms. Wahl continued: *The place where a person resides or is living temporarily does not determine whether they are capable or incapable of respect to some or all decisions they are making. The test of capacity applies to all situations wherever the person lives or is receiving treatment. Just because a person has consented to move to a long-term care facility and required a variety of care services and procedures, there is no automatic implied consent to the process.*[1]

Default Surrogate

The American Bar Association has been trying to define the term "surrogate" in different states. The DEFAULT SURROGATE CONSENT STATUTES July 2017 Explanation: *The descriptors in the chart are generalizations of the statutory language and not quotations, so the statutes must be consulted for precise meaning. The default surrogacy statute language varies from state to state, and the listed descriptors hold the following definitions*:

- Adult includes any person who is 18 years of age or older, is the parent of the child, or has married
- Close friend (adult friend) is the one who has maintained regular contact with the patient as to be familiar with the patient's activities, health, and religious or moral beliefs [4].[2]

What is a healthcare surrogate designation? It is a document naming another person as your representative to make medical decisions for you if you are unable to make them yourself. You can include instructions about any treatment you want or do not want, similar to a living will.[3]

---

[1] Wahl J. The Health Care Consent Act and the Substitute Decisions Act - Who Decides What When? www.acelaw.ca/appimages/file/eamanualsec4c.pdf.

[2] www.americanbar.org.

[3] Florida Advance Directive, www.everplans.com/sites/default/files/Florida_Advance_Directive_Form.pdf.

Surrogate Consent

The application of *surrogate consent* has been applied to particular populations who are unable to meet the requirements necessary to achieve individual informed consent. In this situation, a proxy or patient-designated surrogate is invited to provide substituted judgment based on the patient's known or perceived convictions. However, few discuss their wishes about participating in research in advance, and for populations such as children, the prior discussion is not possible. To protect these people, many suggest the use of surrogate consent only when the proposed research poses minimal risk and the opportunity for direct benefit to the subject.

Compassion and Choices

Compassion and choices work to improve access to a full range of end-of-life options for terminally ill adults, including access to better pain management, palliative care, enrollment in hospice, and aid in dying. Compassion and choices encourage people to document their wishes in an advance directive to ensure that their end-of-life decisions are known.[4]

The policies would be significantly improved by clearly distinguishing between "assisted suicide" and "active euthanasia," which are criminal acts, and the withholding, withdrawing, and refusal of treatment and aid in dying. These clarifications will assist healthcare providers living in jurisdictions where aid in dying is legal to understand

Compassion fatigue has been defined as a combination of physical, emotional, and spiritual depletion associated with caring for patients with significant emotional pain and physical distress.

---

[4] Wegener J, www.forbes.com/sites/kaifalkenberg/2013/01/02/why-rating-your-doctor-is-bad-for-your-health/.

Compassion fatigue has been described among cancer-care providers, emergency room personnel, chaplains, and first responders, among others. This fatigue may impact healthcare providers in any specialty when, in the process of providing empathic support, they experience the pain of their patients and families.

Healthcare Providers

Communicating with family during this process is of utmost importance. In a review of literature conducted by Materstvedt [6], he found that the two main reasons that the patients request assisted dying included loss of dignity and loss of autonomy in their daily life functions at the end of life [2]. A case study reviewed found nothing controversial in a cancer patient's right-to-die decision since it offered a dignified death with relief from suffering. In the state of Oregon, where there are currently right-to-die laws enacted, less than 3% of all deaths were those that were assisted to die [9]. A study that was referenced in Nevidjon and Mayer [3], *reinforced the need for continuing education in end-of-life care and showed the second highest rated core competency needed in communicating about death and dying. It was found that up to 60% percent of patients receiving the end of life care did not feel they were informed entirely of prognosis, the possibility of death or alternatives in communications with their health care providers* [4].

Suggested Reading

1. The Health Care Consent Act and the Substitute Decisions, www.acelaw.ca/appimages/file/eamanualsec4c.pdf.
2. Common Misconceptions about the Substitute Decisions, www.acelaw.ca/appimages/file/25%20Common%20 Misconceptions.pdf.

3. Nevidjon and Mayer. 2012. https:// www.ncbi.nlm.nih.gov/ pubmed/22849013 2012.
4. Default Surrogate Consent Statutes. July 2017. Explanation, www.americanbar.org/content/dam/aba/administrative/ law_aging/2014_default.
5. Living Wills and Advance Directives for Medical Decisions, www.mayoclinic.org/healthy-lifestyle/consumer-health/ in-depth/living-will.
6. Materstvedt. 2013. https://www.ncbi.nlm.nih.gov/ pubmed/24653491
7. Do-Not-Resuscitate Order - Ut Medical Center, www.utmedical-center.org/your-health/encyclopedia/general/carepoint/00047.
8. Tip Sheet # 2 Hierarchy of Substitute Decision Makers, www. acelaw.ca/appimages/file/Tip%20Sheet%20TWO%20-%20 Hierarchy%20of%20SDM.
9. Guerra AL, Frezza EE. To Die or Not to Die: This Is the Dilemma! www.sciforschenonline.org/journals/epidemiology-public-health/article-data/JEPHR-2-138/JEPHR-2-138.pdf.
10. The Health Care Consent Act and Substitute Decisions, www. acelaw.ca/appimages/file/eamanualsec4c.pdf.
11. Frezza EE. *Medical Ethics*. New York: Routledge 2018.

Chapter 23

Long-Term Facilities

The Challenges We Face

The number of older people living in the United States and all around the world is increasing. The secondary effect on healthcare is the need to provide for the people longer, both in and outside the hospital, proving area and facilities that can care for these group of patients and to manage their health and recover from setbacks.[1]

Person-centered care has its focus on providing care that is personalized, enabling, and coordinated for addressing these challenges.[2]

The broader environment within which services are provided is both driving and enabling the development of more person-centered care. Organizations like National Voices (the coalition of health and social care charities) and the Coalition for Collaborative Care (an alliance of major charities and voluntary organizations, professional and leadership bodies in health and social care, and leading development agencies) are driving person-centered practice.[1]

---

[1] http://personcentredcare.health.org.uk/person-centred-care/
overview-of-person-centred-care/why-person-centred-care-important.
[2] www.health.org.uk/publications/person-centred-care-made-simple.

Care Options

The Home Health Care Planning Improvement Act is an amendment to the Act introducing Medicare to revise conditions and limitations on payment for home healthcare services.[3]

Medicare beneficiaries must wait for weeks to see a physician before they get their care covered by Medicare. As a result, patients experience a delay in receiving the care they need. The time delays in getting the correct certification have created backlogs for home health agencies, as well as issues related to billing and payment. To resolve these issues, the Home Health Planning Improvement Act of 2015 (S. 578) was introduced by the Congress.[4]

This act underlines: *Medicare law requires that a physician certify a patient's eligibility for coverage of home health services. Since 1965 when this law was made many older adults now receive care from the mid-level practitioners, such as nurse practitioners and physicians assistants. With the code as it currently reads, a person needing home health services must see a physician (different from their regular provider, say an ARNP) receive home health services.*

This is both inefficient and does not provide good care since neither the physician nor the patients know each other.[5]

Assistance with Activities and Daily Living Needs

From the web page on senior care living, we read: *Activities of Daily Living or ADLs is a term used by healthcare professionals to refer to the basic self-care tasks an individual does on a day-to-day basis. These activities are fundamental in caring for*

---

[3] https://sites.jmu.edu/advocacy/home-health-care-improvement-act/.

[4] www.kantime.com/comprehending-the-home-health-care-improvement-act/.

[5] https://careforce.com/2017/04/04/home-health-care-planning-improvement-act-reintroduced/.

oneself and maintaining independence. An individual's ability or inability to perform ADLs is often used by health professionals as a way of measuring an individual's functional status, especially that of older adults or those with disabilities.[6]

Basic ADLs, sometimes referred to as BADLs, are self-care activities that include the following:

- Mobility: the ability to walk and transfer in and out of a chair or bed
- Personal hygiene
- Oral care and grooming
- Skin and hair care
- Showering and bathing
- Toileting, which includes getting on/off the toilet and cleaning oneself
- Dressing
- Self-feeding.

From Michelle E. Mlinac and Michelle C. Feng,[7] *The ability to perform ADLs and IADLs is dependent upon cognitive (e.g., reasoning, planning), motor (e.g., balance, skill), and perceptual (including sensory) abilities. There is also the important distinction of the individual's ability to complete the task (physical and cognitive ability) versus the ability to recognize that the task needs to be done without prompting (cognitive ability). In many settings, ADLs are directly assessed by occupational, physical or speech therapists, or by nurses and other members of the medical team to guide day-to-day care and as part of discharge planning. ADL capacity assessment often is requested during the middle or later stages of dementia but may also occur during recovery for an acute event like a stroke. Referral for evaluation of ADL ability may include a question*

---

[6] www.seniorliving.org/caregiving/activities-of-daily-living/.

[7] Assessment of activities of daily living, self-care, and independence. *Archives of Clinical Neuropsychology* 2016;31(6): 506–16, https://doi.org/10.1093/arclin/acw049.

*of cognitive, emotional, or behavioral factors that can be inter-
fering with functioning in these basic skills, and how these barriers may be overcome to enhance independence. Also, DSM-5
diagnostic criteria for Major Neurocognitive Disorder specify
that functional impairment with IADLs must be present for
the diagnosis (American Psychiatric Association, 2013). ADL
assessment may also occur as part of a broader capacity evaluation for independent living or guardianship.*

In the long-term activities, it is essential, as we learned from
another website focused on daily living:[8] *The Activities of Daily
Living (ADL's) is a term that is used to describe self-care activities that we perform on a regular daily basis. These include
activities such as bathing, dressing, feeding, grooming, etc. to
name a few. Within the Healthcare Professional realm, the ability or inability to perform the Activities of Daily Living can be a
measurement of a person's function and independence. Care
To Stay Home has designed our services to enhance the dignity
and independence of those who may need assistance with any
Activity of Daily Living.* **Personal Care** *refers to the basic self-
care tasks of bathing, dressing, personal hygiene, and grooming. Personal Care also includes such functions as toileting,
incontinence care, and mobility assistance. Individuals who
begin to need support with one or more of these activities can
benefit from our professionally trained staff.*[9]

Hospice

The word "hospice" first began being used in the mid-1800s
to describe caring for dying patients by Mrs. Jeanne Garnier,
founder of the Dames de Claire in Lyon, France. The Irish Sisters
of Charity adopted it when they opened Our Lady's Hospice
in Dublin, Ireland in 1879 and then again when they began St.
Joseph's Hospice in Hackney, London, England in 1905.[9] At the

---

[8] http://caretostayhome.com/our-services/personal-care-adls/.
[9] www.hindshospice.org/history-of-hospice.html.

end of life, regardless of the disease, there are very few options. For people with cognitive impairment who cannot stay home because they can become dangerous for themselves and others, the hospice is the only option.[10]

The underlying philosophy of hospice focuses on *quality and dignity by providing comfort, care, and support services for people with terminal illnesses and their families. Dementia and Alzheimer are also qualified for hospice.*[11]

The problem is having a sit-down discussion with the family and explaining the reasons medically and ethically. The best would be to talk to the patient themselves if they still can understand and share wishes about life-sustaining treatment.

Hospice care: Care designed to give supportive care to people in the final phase of a terminal illness and focus on comfort and quality of life, rather than cure. The goal is to enable patients to be comfortable and free of pain so that they live each day as entirely as possible.[12]

Routine home care is necessary and includes the following:

■ Nursing services
■ Physician participation
■ Medical social services
■ Home health aide services
■ Counseling services (pastoral, spiritual, bereavement, dietary, and others)
■ Medications
■ Medical equipment
■ Medical supplies
■ Lab and diagnostic studies related to the terminal diagnosis
■ Therapy services.

---

[10] www.nejm.org/doi/full/10.1056/NEJMra1208795
[11] Late-Stage Caregiving|Caregiver Center|Alzheimer's. www.alz.org/care/alzheimers-late-end-stage-caregiving.asp.
[12] Levels of Hospice Care as Defined by Medicare, Top of Form Bottom of Form Angela Morrow, RN May 19, 2018.

If a patient's family is the primary source of care and cannot meet their needs due to caregiver stress or other extenuating circumstances, a patient may temporarily be admitted to an inpatient environment to give the family a needed break.[13]

Home Health

"Home healthcare" implies medical care provided in a patient's home. The care in these structures is given by:

- skilled medical professionals
- skilled nursing care
- physical therapy
- occupational therapy
- speech therapy
- social services
- qualified home health aide.

As the Medicare program describes, *home health care is unique as a care setting not only because the care is provided in the home, but the care itself is "usually less expensive, more convenient, and just as effective" as care given in a hospital or skilled nursing facility. Home Healthcare Data and Readmissions.*[14]

Home Health Services

Home healthcare services include the following:

- Therapy and skilled nursing services
- Administration of medications, including injections
- Medical tests

---

[13] www.verywellhealth.com/levels-of-hospice-care-1132297.

[14] http://ahhqi.org/home-health/what-is.

■ Monitoring of health status
■ Wound care.

Qualification

■ Following hospitalization
■ The transition back to independence
■ Monitoring side effects of a new therapy
■ The overall decline in functioning
■ Learning new skills.

How to Pay for Home Care

■ Private pay
■ Long-term care insurance
■ Medicaid for qualified low-income seniors.

Home Care Services

■ Meal preparation
■ House cleaning
■ Helping dressing, bathing, and grooming
■ Transportation
■ Reminders to take medicine
■ Help with bill paying.[15]

Long-Term Facility

This is a facility that provides rehabilitative, therapeutic, and ongoing skilled nursing care to patients or residents in need of assistance with ADLs.

---

[15] www.aplaceformom.com/planning-and-advice/articles/home-health-vs-home-care.

Long-term care involves a variety of services designed to meet the patients' health or personal care needs during a short or long period when they cannot perform everyday activities on their own.[16]

Long-term care is provided in hospital wards, separate buildings, etc.

The focus is to help in the "ADLs." These activities include bathing, dressing, grooming, using the toilet, eating, and moving around—for example, getting out of bed and into a chair.[17]

People often need long-term care when they have a severe and ongoing health condition or disability. The need for long-term care can arise suddenly, such as after a heart attack or stroke. Most often, however, it develops gradually, as people get older and frailer or as an illness or disability gets worse as in dementia.[17]

Rehabilitation

This is the action of restoring someone to healthy and normal life through training and therapy after illness.

The services may include physical therapy, occupational therapy, speech and language therapy, cognitive therapy, and mental health rehabilitation services.[18]

Subacute-level care is less intensive than acute rehabilitation. In a subacute facility, patients receive between 1 and 2 h of therapy per day. The average length of stay at a subacute facility is also generally longer than at an acute hospital.[19]

---

[16] www.coursehero.com/file/36316094/Longdocx/.

[17] www.nia.nih.gov/health/what-long-term-care.

[18] www.medicinenet.com/script/main/art.asp?articlekey=5288.

[19] www.burke.org/inpatient/admissions/what-is-acute-rehab.

Chapter 24

Comfort Level

Pain Management

According to Diane Glowacki [1], *Effective management of acute pain results in improved patient outcomes and increased patient satisfaction. Although research and advanced treatments in improved practice protocols have documented progressive improvements in the management of acute and postoperative pain, little awareness of the effectiveness of best practices persists. Improved interventions can enhance patients' attitudes to and perceptions of pain. What a patient believes and understands about pain is critical in influencing the patient's reaction to the pain therapy provided. Use of interdisciplinary pain teams can lead to improvements in patients' pain management, pain education, outcomes, and satisfaction. Adequate pain management enhances earlier mobility and lessens the complications of ileus, urinary retention, and myocardial infarction. Sleep deprivation, which can increase postoperative fatigue, resulting in decreased mobility, is also reduced, as are pulmonary complications.*

On the other side, Nancy Wells, Chris Pasero, and Margo McCaffery [2] reported: *Continuous, unrelieved pain also affects the psychological state of the patient and family members. Common psychological responses to pain include anxiety and depression. The inability to escape from pain may create a sense of helplessness and even hopelessness, which may predispose the patient to a more chronic depression. Patients who have experienced inadequate pain management may be reluctant to seek medical care for other health problems."* Diana Grabowski reported instead that despite considerable achievement, pain control is still a main goal in health care (https://www.aacn.org/docs/cemedia/C1533.pdf) [3].

In a previous paper [4], JCAHO underlines that *Poorly managing pain may put clinicians at risk for legal action. Current standards for pain management, such as the national standards outlined by the Joint Commission (formerly known as the Joint Commission on Accreditation of Healthcare Organizations, JCAHO), require that pain is promptly addressed and managed.*

Having standards of care in place increases the risk of legal action against clinicians and institutions for inadequate pain management, and there are instances of lawsuits filed for insufficient pain management by physicians. Nurses, as part of the collaborative team responsible for managing pain during hospitalization, also may be liable for legal action [5].

According to Bair [6], *Hospitals stand to lose reputation as well as profit if the pain is poorly managed. Patient satisfaction with care is strongly tied to their experiences with pain during hospitalization. Evidence indicates that higher levels of anxiety and depression are linked to poor satisfaction with care in ambulatory settings. With the advent of transparent health care, report cards for hospitals are becoming more prevalent, and performance on pain management is likely to be one of the indicators reported.*

Make Them Understand the Hospital Surroundings and Environment

The hospital's physical layout and ambiance can have a significant effect on patient outcomes and recovery times. Factors such as space, lighting, use of color, acoustics, noise levels, smell, and the degree of control a patient has over their environment can all have an impact on the well-being and mood of the individual.

Strengthening the bond between the working environment and the staff can increase the levels of satisfaction, thus improving patient care. The healthcare staff is directly affected by the hospital design, in particular, the physical layouts and interior ambiance related to communication, productivity, and team working [7].

Patricia Stones reported: *A growing number of studies in health care show that members of organizations are more satisfied when they work in climates that have more supportive and empowering leadership and organizational arrangements, along with more positive group environments (often reflecting elements of group support and collaboration). Moreover, although the research base is not as strong, there is emerging evidence that these same organizational attributes impact employee turnover and, most important, patient safety. Improving the regulatory climate is likely to improve patient safety and decrease overall health care costs. However, future research studying specific interventions and their cost-effectiveness are needed* [8].

Suggested Reading

1. Glowacki D. Effective pain management and improvements in patients' outcomes and satisfaction. *Crit Care Nurse* 2015; 35(3):33–41.

2. Wells N, Pasero C, McCaffery M. Improving the quality of care through pain assessment and management. Chapter 17 In: *Patient Safety and Quality: An Evidence-Based Handbook for Nurses*, www.ncbi.nlm.nih.gov/books/NBK2658/.

3. Furrow BR. Pain management and provider liability: No more excuses. *J Law Med Ethics* 2001;29(1):28–51.

4. Joint Commission on Accreditation of Healthcare Organizations, JCAHO. *Comprehensive Hospital Accreditation Manual.* Oakbrook Terrace, IL: JCAHO; 2001.

5. D'Arcy Y. Pain management standards, the law, and you. *Nursing* 2005;35(4):17.

6. Bair MJ, Kroenke K, Sutherland JM, McCoy KD, Harris H, McHorney CA. Effects of depression and pain severity on satisfaction in medical outpatients: Analysis of the Medical Outcomes Study. *J Rehabil Res Dev* 2007;44(2):143–52.

7. www.theguardian.com/sustainable-business/hospital-environment-affect-patients-staff.

8. Stone PW, Hughes R, Dailey M. Creating a safe and high-quality health care environment. In: *Patient Safety and Quality: An Evidence-Based Handbook for Nurses.* www.ncbi.nlm.nih.gov/books/NBK2634/.

9. Frezza EE. *Medical Ethics.* New York: Routledge Publishing 2018.

Chapter 25

Chronic Conditions and Pain Management

Chronic conditions need different expertise and training most of the time, and they represent a complex medical puzzle.

Examples are general medicine and geriatric medicine. Geriatric medicine, which was initially incorporated into general practice, is now becoming a science and specialty on its own, given the complexity of the medical issues and the fact that the population lives longer and new challenges have been discovered.

Since the diseases are different, the patients are different, and with age, their responses to medicine are different. Similarly for chronic illness, the patient is different and takes more time.[1]

Hospital System

Dedicate social workers and case managers to set up long-term facilities and home care to set up authorizations, etc.

---

[1] www.healthcommunities.com/health-care-providers/what-is-a-geriatrician.shtml.

Experts and Expertise

We need more trained healthcare professionals, which involve capable and skilled staff. We need expert and expertise. Here we give three examples of conditions. These should be not considered as a medical suggestions since the book is not a medical book but an idea of what to do to place patients first.

Clinical Examples

Atherosclerosis Care

The first treatment of atherosclerosis is lifestyle changes—eat better and exercise more. Medication is the cornerstone in the control of blood pressure and/or cholesterol levels.

Surgical procedures may be recommended in a specific situation to avoid complete occlusion or to reopen occluded vessels.[2]

Cholesterol medications. Aggressively lowering your low-density lipoprotein cholesterol, the "bad" cholesterol, can slow, stop, or even reverse the buildup of fatty deposits in your arteries. Boosting your high-density lipoprotein cholesterol, the "good" cholesterol, may help, too.

Antiplatelet medications. Antiplatelet medications, such as aspirin, to reduce the likelihood that platelets will clump in narrowed arteries, form a blood clot, and cause further blockage.

Beta-blocker medications. These medications are commonly used for coronary artery disease. They lower your heart rate and blood pressure, reducing the demand on your heart, and often relieve symptoms of chest pain. Beta-blockers reduce the risk of heart attacks and some heart rhythm problems.[3]

---

[2] www.sciencecare.com/what-is-atherosclerosis-and-what-causes-it/.
[3] www.healthline.com/health/heart-disease/beta-blockers.

Angiotensin-converting enzyme (ACE) inhibitors. These medications may help slow the progression of athero-sclerosis by lowering blood pressure and producing other beneficial effects on the heart arteries. ACE inhibitors can also reduce the risk of recurrent heart attacks.

Calcium channel blockers. These medications lower blood pressure and are sometimes used to treat angina.

Diuretics. High blood pressure is a significant risk factor for atherosclerosis—diuretics lower blood pressure.

Chronic Obstructive Pulmonary Disease Care

Chronic obstructive pulmonary disease (COPD) is a condition in which the airways in the lungs become damaged, making it increasingly difficult for air to move in and out.

Two important kinds of damage can cause COPD:

- The airways in the lungs become scarred and narrowed
- The air sacs in the lung, where oxygen is absorbed into the blood and carbon dioxide is excreted, become damaged.

Also, COPD is often associated with inflammation of the airways that can lead to cough and production of phlegm (sputum). When the damage is severe, it may become difficult to get enough oxygen into the blood and to get rid of excess carbon dioxide. These changes lead to shortness of breath and other symptoms.[4]

Unfortunately, the signs of COPD cannot be eliminated with treatment and the condition usually worsens over time. However, treatment can control symptoms and can sometimes slow the progression of the disease. Treatment options for people with COPD need to be discussed seriously with an expert.

---

[4] www.coursehero.com/file/32346761/Patient-educationdocx/.

Depression Care

The American Psychiatric Association recently updated its guidelines[5] on the treatment of major depressive disorder. *The new evidence-based guideline summarizes recommendations on the use of antidepressants and other drug therapies; psychotherapy, including cognitive behavior therapy; and electroconvulsive therapy (ECT). Because many patients with the major depressive disorder have co-occurring psychiatric disorders, including substance use disorders, physicians should also consider appropriate treatments for these diagnoses. Patients who have depressive symptoms in the context of another disorder but who do not meet the diagnostic criteria for major depressive disorder should be treated according to guidelines about the primary diagnosis.*

Dedicate an End-of-Life Team

The definition for palliative care is taken from the NIH page[6]: *palliative care consultation team is a multidisciplinary team that works with the patient, family, and the patient's other doctors to provide medical, social, emotional, and practical support. The team is made of palliative care specialist doctors and nurses and includes others such as social workers, nutritionists, and chaplains.*

Critical Status

The legal involvement in medical ethics as it pertains to the continuation of care in the intensive care unit indeed became evident in 1972 with the definition of the persistent vegetative state, which began finding its way into legal documents and courtroom vernacular. Other terms followed, such as imminent

---

[5] www.aafp.org/afp/2011/0515/p1219.html.

[6] www.nia.nih.gov/health/what-are-palliative-care-and-hospice-care.

death—death despite maximum medical therapy. Irreversible death—susceptible to palliation but permanently incapacitating to mind and body and ultimately fatal.

Other vital definitions include that of death—irreversible neurologic arrest and cardiopulmonary arrest. In 1990, the patient self-determination act went into law giving rise to living wills—defined primarily as instructions to healthcare workers for the end of life. An advanced directive transfers the act of dying from a natural action to a deed. It hastens death, but not causes death, and it transforms the moment of death into a matter of judgment—therefore, a negotiated death. The AMA in 2016[7] published its principles at the end of life, which described that *life should be cherished despite disabilities and handicaps, except when the prolongation would be inhumane and criminal. Under these circumstances withholding or withdrawing life-sustaining therapies is ethical provided that the standard care given an individual who is ill is not discontinued. The American College of Surgeons*[8] *developed and published a position on do not resuscitate (DNR) in 2014 mainly as it pertains to the operating room—surgeons must take the lead role with at least part of the discussion describing that many routine aspects of anesthesia are identical to resuscitative activities such as intubation.*

Opioid Crisis

From the commission of the Congress notes,[9] the committee had to mandate educational initiatives at medical and dental schools to tighten opioid prescribing, and funding a program to expand access to medications used to treat addictions.

---

[7] www.ama-assn.org/delivering-care/ethics/
code-medical-ethics-caring-patients-end-life.

[8] www.facs.org/about-acs/statements/19-advance-directives.

[9] President Trump May Declare Opioid Epidemic... from www.npr.org/2017/10/26/560083795/president-trump-may-declare-opioid-epidemic.

The Congress is currently spending $500 million a year on addiction treatment programs, but that money runs out the next year.

Another option from the Congress notes would be to restore a funding cut proposed for Substance Abuse and Mental Health Services Administration, the agency within the Department of Health and Human Services that oversees addiction treatment programs. In its 2018 budget, the Trump administration proposed cutting the agency's budget by nearly $400 million.[9]

Classification of Pain

There are three primary sources of pain:

Physiological: Nociceptive and neuropathic
Etiologic: Malignant or nonmalignant
Temporal: Sopra tentorial.

Why Patients Seek Medications

There are different reasons why the patient seeks medication:

1. Runs out of medicine early
2. "Loses" medications
3. Requests specific medication
4. Claims "allergies"
5. Reports no relief with other treatments
6. Does not comply with other therapies
7. Refuses urine drug screens.

Chronic Pain—The Rising Problem

Opioid abuse rose dramatically between 1997 and 2007. There are few points to make on the increasing number of chronic pain cases.

1. The cost of chronic pain now exceeds those of cancer, diabetes, and heart disease combined in the United States
2. Around 50 million Americans suffer from chronic pain
3. About 70% are undertreated
4. The United States, with approximately 5% of the world's population, consumes 99% of the world's hydrocodone.

Unfortunately, we are not ready since the physicians often struggle with ethical issues in pain management. Therefore, the undertreatment of pain has increased as both a *public health* problem and a *human rights* issue.

The physicians have been asked to be moral and legal gatekeepers in identifying legitimate pain patients. That started with medical school, since the medical school curriculum now rarely includes governmental regulation of pain management. For instance, 51% of Texas physicians believe that prescribing long-acting opioids will lead to patient addiction.

A survey done in 2011 Hambleton reported the following:

1. The decrease in prescription drug abuse in children and young adults
2. Only 19% of surveyed physicians received any medical school training in drug diversion and only 40% in substance use disorders
3. About 43% do not ask about prescription drug abuse and diversion
4. Old records are not obtained by 33% before prescribing controlled substances

5. Around 66% of the Texas family physicians are anxious about prescribing opioids for chronic pain.[10]

Pain is the number one reason why patients visit medical facilities. Various approaches have been tried to encourage patients and physicians to talk about and to allow for adequate treatment. Every time a patient looks suspicious, they should be placed automatically in the database to control substance to prevent medicine shopping.

Finally how we define a suspicious patient, that patient does is abusive of the system?

- Complains about excessive pain compared to clinical finding
- Takes more medication than is needed
- Calls office for more prescription
- Does not pay for the visit.

---

[10] Hambleton. 2013. *Morbidity and Mortality Weekly Report* 49(23): June 28, 2010.

Chapter 26

Dignity in Dementia

Involving patients in decision-making is essential to achieve the goal of maintaining dignity in dementia patients. We must recognize that they are individuals with unique values and preferences. The patients must be treated with dignity, respecting their cultural values and autonomy, particularly in the presence of dementia.

Dementia

People with cognitive changes caused by mild cognitive impairment (MCI) have an increased risk of developing Alzheimer's or dementia. However, not all people with MCI develop Alzheimer's.[1]

The issue of dementia from the ethics point of view is to understand both the provider (physician, nurses, etc.) and the caregiver (family and proxy). The healthcare provider has some experience in treating dementia patients, but the family does not. They get involved in the direct care of a patient for the first time, who in this case could be one of the family members, such as a parent most of the time, or a husband or wife.

---

[1] www.alz.org/alzheimers-dementia/stages.

The patient is in the middle and most of the time is forgotten—it is most important that we do not lose the focus on dignity. Yes, the dignity of these people with cognitive impairment is of utmost importance.

Aligning Providers and Family

It is of utmost importance that the physician and all team explain and ask about the feelings and the issues the family has. More often the focus is on the patient, and we forget about the family that needs to cope with a person that all of a sudden seems like his soul is not there anymore! It happened to me with my father.

I did not have any support; even though I was a physician, I did not know what to do. I had to learn on my own through different web pages. My mother, who wasn't computer-friendly, was left even more alone than me. What do you do when the patient wakes up in the middle of the night and tries to get you out of "his house" because he does not recognize you? My mother was locked out of the house and had to call the police to get back in. How can you call a person down when they have the hallucinations? Most of the time they do not want to take the medications or they hide them.

I never thanked my mother enough for being able to perform a job which is commonly done in hospice by multiple providers.

Well, the process is long and painful, and you always have the hope that it will reverse, but the stages of Alzheimer's are quite common and repeat themselves in different people.

The family most often feels:

■ the notion of "conscience" as underpinning his duty to care
■ aligned with the sense of duty and responsibility and a sense of guilt

- the need to justify their acts of deceiving the person with dementia into believing different things, with the intent to help
- reciprocity, by ignoring his previously expressed wishes
- not appreciated for the strain of caring.

I had never realized the strain that a patient with cognitive impairment could bring to the family until I had my own experience. There is some point that the researcher made about this.

A family living with Alzheimer's will face many decisions throughout the disease stages, including decisions about care, treatment, participation in research, end-of-life issues, autonomy, and safety.

First, they do not realize how much care they need, and during the late stages, this can excite what they can provide at home even with assistance.

The trauma of moving a person to a facility is on both sides—the patient and the family.

The decisions in the late stages become more pressing and more difficult to make, and some families are not ready. They need to get through, but they always end up second-guessing their initial decisions.

Dignity of Care

At the end of life, regardless of the disease, there are very few options for people with cognitive impairment who cannot stay home because they become dangerous for themselves and others. In such cases, the hospice is the only option.

The underlying philosophy of hospice focuses on quality and dignity by providing comfort, care, and support services for people with terminal illnesses and their families. To qualify for hospice benefits under Medicare, a physician must diagnose the person with Alzheimer's disease as having less than 6 months to live.[2]

The problem is having a sit-down discussion with the family and explaining the reasons medically and ethically. The best option will be to talk to the patient itself if he still can comprehend and share wishes about life-sustaining treatment.

As cognitive abilities decline, respect for the autonomy of the person with dementia will conflict with the ethical considerations of taking away a person's right to autonomous decision-making.

The healthcare provider must also be trained in taking care of these patients; just showing up to work is not enough. Hospice needs to have specific training for the providers and the physician should look at the quality care of these facilities. Often, the people that work in these services are not trained; they do not know what the disease can bring, and most of all, they lack compassion.

They also need to have the personnel to help family member cope. For example, a couple that gets separated by the disease all of a sudden after many years of togetherness is a significant trauma for the one that is still sane. This can create disorder and psychological impairment in the person that needs to be strong to help the patient in this time of the lifespan.

The system needs to be set in a way to understand what is going on with the patients to cope and to give the best treatment, which in this case, starts with the family.

All they need at the end of the stages is the dignity of care, which will be our ethical duty to them.

Suggested Reading

1. Stages of Alzheimer's & Symptoms|Alzheimer's Association, www.alz.org/alzheimers_disease_stages_of_alzheimers. asp?type=alzchptfoot.

---

[2] www.alz.org/help-support/caregiving/financial-legal-planning/medicare.

2. Late-Stage Caregiving|Caregiver Center|Alzheimer's, www.alz. org/care/alzheimers-late-end-stage-caregiving.asp.
3. Frezza EE. *Medical Ethics.* New York: Routledge Publishing; 2018.
4. Hughes JC, Hope T, Savulescu J, Ziebland S. Carers, ethics, and dementia: A survey and review of the literature. *Int J Geriatr Psychiatry* 2002;17:35–40.
5. Hughes JC. Views of the person with dementia. *J Med Ethics* 2001;27:86–91.
6. Pratt C, Schmall V, Wright S. Ethical concerns of family caregivers to dementia patients. *Gerontologist* 1987;27:632–8.
7. Parsons K. The male experience of caregiving for a family member with Alzheimer's disease. *Qual Health Res* 1997;7:391–407.
8. Pinner G. Truth-telling and the diagnosis of dementia. *Br J Psychiatry* 2000;176:514–15.
9. Kitwood T. *Dementia Reconsidered. The Person Comes First.* Buckingham: Open University Press; 1997:91.
10. Sabat SR, Harré R. The Alzheimer's disease sufferer as a semiotic subject. *Philosophy Psychiatry Psychol* 1994;1:145–60.
11. Schneider J, Murray J, Banerjee S, Mann A. Eurocare: A cross-national study of co-resident spouse carers for people with Alzheimer's disease: I—factors associated with carer burden. *Int J Geriat Psychiatry* 1999;14:651–61.
12. Fulford KWM. *Moral Theory and Medical Practice.* Cambridge: Cambridge University Press; 1989.

BUILDING QUALITY SYSTEMS

Chapter 27

Patient Flow and Press Ganey Scores

Minimize Waiting Time

Mastering the patient flow starts with better organized scheduling to minimize waiting time. Every office is supposed to have a system in place. Let's review some of the time issues and ranges.

- Time to walk in the office for registration: 10–15 min
- Time from registration to the room: 10–15 min
- Time from being in the place to nurse visit for vitals: 5–10 min
- Time from vitals to physician visit: 10–15 min
- Time from end visit with doctor to check out—depending on the goal and assessment: <30 min.

Scheduling

It is not a secret that scheduling is the most critical factor. The patient visits should be planned appropriately.

It means that the patient should be scheduled for the right amount of time. This cannot be done by merely leaving it to the front office; the doctor needs to be involved in it. The physician should give specific time. Different patients require a different setup. For instance, for a surgeon, a new patient will require more time than a postoperative patient. But a postoperative patient that has stitches or stapler or drainages to take out will take longer than a patient without those needs. Therefore, the physician needs to be directly involved with the schedule.

Optimize Time in Office

To optimize the time, an electronic medical system can be helpful—a monitor like the one in the airport to tell everyone when the patient has arrived, has registered in the room, is with the physician, etc.

Color-coded systems have been used in some offices, but at times the color does not match between providers from the same office and that can be confusing. Confusion is definitely not part of competent patient-centered care goals.

Standardization of color and system is needed across the border, across offices and states.

Mastering Patient Flow

The book *Mastering Patient Flow* by Elizabeth Woodcock[1] has impressively summarized quite well the different stages of physician practice. The quality care of patients can be increased by a simple adjustment of the physician's time. Do we know how difficult it is to achieve the goal? It is true that if you are not careful about the time spent in between patients,

---

[1] *Mastering Patient Flow*, MGMA, 2nd edition; 2003.

on doing other things that are not patient related, at the end of the year, they add up, and you are decreasing your patient contact.

It is true as well that the only way now to do a quality practice is to see patients on time and well. Everything else in the office is a standard fixed process that cannot change. The ability to use a resource to increase the value of your service is essential, and a physician has to know when they don't use their time correctly. It is critical to try to satisfy patients because that is the key to a successful practice. Another interesting concept is to monitor other physicians. Most of the time, when physicians come into practice, they make a list of things to do for their own and forget that they work for training, and therefore, they tend to see fewer patients and spend less time with them. This will never work since it results either in reduced cash flow or in reduced patient quality impact.

Are you going solo? I tried to go solo myself, and it was not a good experience. The fixed costs in my practice ended up going so high that the reimbursement for each service was not paying enough.

Phone Services

Not only the patient contacts but also the most uncomplicated services can be a hurdle for the patients and create confusion and poor-quality services. Let's take the example of phone services. It is interesting how a telephone can be a friend or foe for us.

To start my own practice, I would like to get an interactive voice recognition on my phone and put a list of people to contact. For example, if you want to reach somebody, press zero and not a long list of numbers because that makes it very confusing for the patient. We have to use it wisely, such as pressing one to schedule an appointment, two to speak with a nurse, three to discuss a bill, four to refill a prescription, five to talk to an operator, and that is it because that will be already enough. I prefer the computer-generated calls for scheduling. It takes a lot of time and effort from the patient as well as staff.

Advanced Assets Concept

1. Allow last-minute appointments. It is healthy to have a full schedule with few spots for last-minute appointments. It seems that for the good name of the practice, it is always good to have time in the schedule to see patients at the last minute. This will increase the patient's satisfaction and make the staff happy as well, since they do not have to receive extra phone calls from the same patient to be scheduled over and over. You practice wisely, and you use your resources wisely

2. It is important to reinforce. This includes *standard window fees*, including communicating policies for no show with costs that can vary from $25 to $35. The so-called *bumping*, that is, the physician changes the schedule, should be avoided

3. Be careful on registrations. Registrations can take a long time, and redoing them even longer!

4. No bumping. On the other side, it is essential for the physician not to change the schedule to make it easy for the front desk

5. Decrease waiting time. Patient waiting should be 10–20 min and not longer, because otherwise, the patient can choose another practice

6. Make the waiting room comfortable. There needs to be an area where the patient is at ease and can wait a few minutes before going to the office

7. Make the next appointment right away. Avoid extra phone calls. The visit should be smooth sailing; this will avoid additional phone calls. The new appointment will be given right after the tour—the charge before the trip

8. All-inclusive visit. Have labs and X-ray in the office for more compliance
9. Decision. In the end, a decision about the treatment needs to be made and shared with the patients to engage them in their healthcare
10. Obtaining insurance date. It is of utmost importance to have patients insurances and obtain insurance clearing before procedures or another visit. This can take between 7 and 28 days.

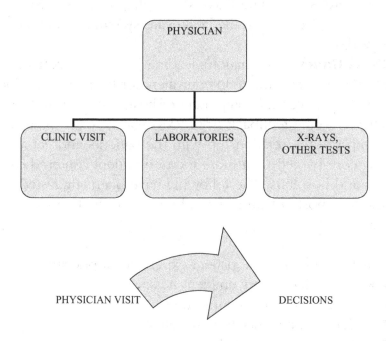

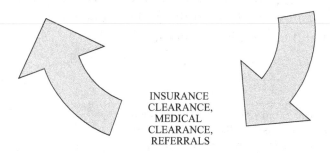

Press Ganey Scores

This is a patient experience company in South Bend, Indiana. It is an independent company. This means less bias in the survey questions or reported results. Press Ganey partners with more than 50% of all U.S. hospitals to help improve clinical and business outcomes.

The score is intended to help hospitals see what areas need to be improved to enhance the patient experience. The Press Ganey score is important because it highlights those processes or services within the healthcare system that need to be reviewed.[2]

Press Ganey is the nation's leading provider of patient satisfaction surveys, the Yelp equivalent for hospitals and doctors, and is the central component of healthcare reform.[3]

Thanks to the feedback from Press Ganey scores, we can now improve the relationship with the patients and get a better score by getting a more focused patient-centered care clinics and hospitals. The following have been suggested to be the five most critical steps to be taken to make the scores better:

- Make improving the patient experience a priority
- Reduce unnecessary ambient noise
- Streamline staff communication
- Understand patients' time sensitivity
- Keep patients informed.

The interesting part is that most of the Press Ganey scores subjects are now the base of the patient-centered care approach and tackled in this book.

---

[2] www.medbizmag.com/press-ganey-score-important/.
[3] www.forbes.com/sites/kaifalkenberg/2013/01/02/
why-rating-your-doctor-is-bad-for-your-health/.

Suggested Reading

1. Stewart M, Brown JB, Donner A, McWhinney IR, Oates J, Weston WW, Jordan J. The impact of patient-centered care on outcomes. *J Fam Pract* 2000;49:796–804.
2. Levenstein JH, McCracken EC, McWhinney IR, Stewart MA, Brown JB. The patient-centered clinical method: I. A model for the doctor-patient interaction in family medicine. *Fam Pract* 1986;3:24–30.
3. Stewart AL, Hays RD, Ware JE. The MOS short-form general health survey. *Med Care* 1988;26:724–35.
4. Brown JB, Weston WW, Stewart MA. Patient-centered interviewing: Part II. *Can Fam Physician* 1989;35:153–57.
5. Stewart M, Weston WW, Brown JB, McWhinney IR, McWilliam CL, Freeman TR. *Patient-Centered Medicine: Transforming the Clinical Method.* Thousand Oaks, CA: Sage Publications; 1995:21.
6. Brown JB, Stewart M, Tessier S. Assessing communication between patients and doctors: A manual for scoring patient-centered communication. Working Paper Series #95-2. London, Canada: The University of Western Ontario; 1995.
7. Brown J, Stewart MA, McCracken EC, McWhinney IR, Levenstein JH. The patient-centered clinical method. 2. Definition and application. *Fam Pract* 1986;3:75–9.
8. Stewart M, Brown J, Levenstein J, McCracken E, McWhinney IR. The patient-centered clinical method. 3. Changes in residents' performance over two months of training. *Fam Pract* 1986;3:164–7.

Chapter 28

Clinical Staff and Better Patient Experience

Staffing

Every practice seeks to find the right staffing ration for the best patient flow in the office and the hospital to run the most productive business. Medical practices that are highly productive already understand the principles of good staffing, says Marc Halley, president and CEO of The Halley Consulting Group: *They may not call it "highest and best-use staffing" but that's what they're practicing.*[1] In the highest and best-used staffing model, the primary roles do only what is in their job description and nothing else. For example, a physician should practice medicine, not just fill out paperwork or make copies, Halley says.[2]

The clinical assistant has two critical roles:

1. Ensuring that the patient has a high-quality experience
2. Driving and managing the physician's productivity by focusing on one exam room and one individual at a time.

---

[1] Halley. *MGMA 2010 Annual Conference.*
[2] www.psychiatry.org/patients-families/depression/what-is-depression.

A 2010 Medical Group Management Association (MGMA) *e-Source article* addressed how to approach this second role for nursing staff. If you still seek that perfect model, there are three primary roles affecting office qualities:

1. The physician
2. The clinical assistant
3. The receptionist.

Halley says: *the rest of the practice, including administrators, are in secondary parts and should support the primary functions in meeting the needs, wants and priorities of referring physicians and patients.*

Clinical Staff

Generally, the clinical staff consist of either licensed personnel (registered nurses [RNs], licensed practical nurses [LPNs], etc.) and non-licensed personnel (medical, nursing, and medical surgical assistants [MAs, CNAs, SAs]). If your clinical model demands that the staff make a lot of critical decisions and perform various medical procedures, you'll want more licensed professionals. The clinical team cannot focus solely on driving physicians' patient flow and making essential choices if they're on the phone with an insurance carrier or a pharmacy. To solve this common problem, more staff may be necessary. In fact, *many of the highest-producing practices in the country have more full-time-equivalent (FTE) support staff per physician than those who are producing at a lower level.* Halley reported in his MGMA 2009 *Performance and Practices of Successful Medical Groups Report* that the median total support staff FTE per physician is 5.24 for "better performers" versus 4.43 for the "others."

How Many FTEs

One of the factors that need to be considered is what jobs we're talking about -- clinical or front office. It's staffing in the clinical area that will do most to enhance the clinic flow, so that's what we'll focus on in this discussion. Another thing to consider is a specialty since some specialists can get by with far fewer support staff than others.[3]

Rosemarie Nelson further reported: *Most practices think they need to be lean and mean, yet all too often that means understaffing! The more profitable practices generally have more staff per full-time equivalent (FTE) physician. The following table is from "Performances and Practices of Successful Medical Groups: 2009 Report Based on 2008 Data" published by the Medical Group Management Association (MGMA). It demonstrates the consistently higher ratio of support staff to physicians in better performing practices. Note: the numbers presented here are for total FTEs, including both clinical and nonclinical support staff.*[4]

Table Summarized: Consistently Higher Ratio of Support Staff to Physicians in Better Performing Practices

But you cannot focus on the FTE count only! You have to understand the impact that headcount has on operations. Rosemarie Nelson also looked at the key performance indicators. Median per FTE physician demonstrates that the practices using an electronic health record (EHR) have a higher ratio of support staff per FTE physician than other methods while

---

[3] Nelson R. www.medpagetoday.com/columns/practicepointers/22099.

[4] Nelson R. How much Staff should the Doctor have? www.kevinmd.com/blog/2010/10/staff-doctor.html.

	FTEs		Charges	
Multispecialty	5.24	4.43	$321,894	$216,515
Orthopedic surgery	7.70	5.49	$642,572	$537,266
Cardiology	6.86	5.41	$675,977	$504,676
Primary care – single specialties	4.56	3.50	$242,142	$136,479
Surgical – single specialties	5.95	3.54	$558,533	$445,618
Medicine – single specialties exc. General Med.	5.61	3.09	$550,185	$379,237

Source: Modified from Nelson R, www.kevinmd.com/blog/2010/10/staff-doctor.html.

generating a more significant percentage of medical revenue after operating cost.

Facility Resources

Staffing and productivity are also dependent on resources. Usually, the physician has one assistant assigned for the day and that nurse is responsible for all the clinical support throughout the patient flow.

The physician is frustrated—the wait time cannot be billed, and the frustration of the physician can bring the provider to leave the organization. If the physician is additionally supported by a float nurse or shares a nurse with another physician, downtime could be minimized, the patient wait time could be reduced, and the nurse who is doing the intake—will be able to complete the information process faster and minimize the downtime.[3]

Add another medical assistant to the headcount (approximately $32,000 annual salary and benefits) and generate more revenue (roughly $46,000 net income for two additional patients per block time). This is without calculating the indirect benefits by decreasing waiting time to obtain a better-quality evaluation and better insurance contracts and more referral.

As we reported in Chapter 27, the office does not score on the physical ability but 75% on the office itself. So get the office moving; get a clean, efficient office. Even if people think it does not make money, your relationship and your efficiency will be proven from better referral and better insurance contracts, and most of all patients' satisfaction and Press Ganey scores.

How to Calculate the Clinic Income and Adjust the Number of FTEs?

Following is the list of the data you need to get:

- Average clinic patients per day (week or month)
- Gross charges × visit × patient per day
- Average collection × visit
- Total revenue × work relative value unit (RVU)
- How many patients seen per day?
- How many collections per day?
- Total collection for each physician (divide into technical and clinic collections)
- How many FT's total in the clinic
- Specify degree (RN, MA, license vocational nurse (LVN), etc., secretary)
- Gross salary for clinic FT's
- Allot time for visit: New vs Established = 15 vs 30 min
- Time for patient sign in, patient seen, patient sign out (throughput output of the clinic).

Formulas

1. Physician gross charges excluding technical component divided for the patient
2. Average charge × visit = $1,599 for general surgery

3. Gross revenue × Wrvu = $128
4. Annual collection × visit = $450 (influenced by payer mix).

The following table is from "Performances and Practices of Successful Medical Groups: 2009 Report Based on 2008 Data" published by MGMA. *It demonstrates the consistently higher ratio of support staff to physicians in better performing practices. Note: the numbers presented here are for total FTEs, including both clinical and nonclinical support staff.*[4]

	Staff FTEs per FTE MD Better Performers	Staff FTEs per FTE MD Other Practices	Medical Rvenue after Operating and net Cost per FTE MD Better Performers	Medical Revenue after Operating and NPP Cost per FTE MD Other Practices
Multispecialty	5.24	4.43	$321,894	$216,515
Orthopedic surgery	7.70	5.49	$642,572	$537,266
Cardiology	6.86	5.41	$675,977	$504,676
Primary care — single specialties	4.56	3.50	$242,142	$136,479
Surgical — single specialties	5.95	3.54	$558,533	$445,618
Medicine — single specialties exc. General Med.	5.61	3.09	$550,185	$379,237

Source: Rosemarie Nelson is a principal with the MGMA Health Care Consulting Group, 2010-09-09T13:59:17-0400.

Clinic Staffing and Ratio

Synopsis

1 LVN or LPN (license practice nurse: training in the clinic)

MA has more undefined role which varies according to state law

1 LVN 1 MA for 15–20 patients per shift

Busy surgeon; 40 patients per clinic day; 1 LVN; 1 Scriba.

Eight interventional cardiology group: 1 RN who can supervise, 8 MA under the RN, taking care of 15–20 patients a day per physician

Family Practice physician = 2 FTs for 24 patients a day.

National Average Office FTE Numbers

Nurse FTE: 13.3
Tech FTE: 5.4
Administrative FTE: 8.5
Administrator FTE: 1.0
Total FTE: 27.6

Based on Location

West
Nurse FTE: 10.9
Tech FTE: 4.9
Administrative FTE: 8.1
Administrator FTE: 1.0
Total FTE: 26.3

Southwest
Nurse FTE: 11.4
Tech FTE: 4.8
Administrative FTE: 7.6
Administrator FTE: 1.0
Total FTE: 24.5

Midwest
　Nurse FTE: 13.4
　Tech FTE: 4.6
　Administrative FTE: 7.3
　Administrator FTE: 1.0
　Total FTE: 27.2
Southeast
　Nurse FTE: 12.1
　Tech FTE: 5.0
　Administrative FTE: 7.7
　Administrator FTE: 1.0
　Total FTE: 26.8
Northeast
　Nurse FTE: 10.9
　Tech FTE: 3.9
　Administrative FTE: 7.1
　Administrator FTE: 1.0
　Total FTE: 23.4

Based on the Hospital Operating Room Size

1–2 ORs (operating rooms)
　Nurse FTE: 7.6
　Tech FTE: 2.5
　Administrative FTE: 5.1
　Administrator FTE: 1.0
　Total FTE: 16.0
3–4 ORs
　Nurse FTE: 11.5
　Tech FTE: 4.4
　Administrative FTE: 7.5
　Administrator FTE: 1.0
　Total FTE: 24.5
More than 4 ORs
　Nurse FTE: 16.7
　Tech FTE: 7.5

Administrative FTE: 10.1
Administrator FTE: 1.0
Total FTE: 35.9

Based on the Hospital Operating Room Volume

Less than 3,000 annual cases
Nurse FTE: 6.9
Tech FTE: 2.5
Administrative FTE: 4.4
Administrator FTE: 1.0
Total FTE: 14.6
3,000–5,999 annual cases
Nurse FTE: 10.2
Tech FTE: 4.3
Administrative FTE: 7.1
Administrator FTE: 1.0
Total FTE: 22.3
More than 5,999 annual cases
Nurse FTE: 15.0
Tech FTE: 6.1
Administrative FTE: 9.3
Administrator FTE: 1.0
Total FTE: 31.2

Chapter 29

Fall Prevention— Engaging the Family

Fall Prevention

From the medical and surgical floor to the emergency department and the outpatient departments, the risk of fall is always around the corner. This does not depend upon their diseases but upon the situation they are in, such as stress, confusion, uncomfortable bed, need to go to the bathroom, and feeling imprisoned. All of these and others can be the reasons why the patient accidentally stands and tries to walk, but because they are unwell they lose their balance and fall.

Falling is a significant problem for hospitals and personnel, and it is a sentinel reportable episode. Therefore, most of the hospitals have been trying to implement policies to get better patient care. In most of these cases, it is not possible to share the vision with the patients since they are confused, and therefore, rules need to be in place to protect the patients.

Fall prevention and risk interventions that are implemented should be documented in the electronic medical record or an appropriate downtime form.

An environmental assessment should be conducted for all patients during purposeful rounds for patient safety.

Definition of Falls

Patient Fall

A fall is an unplanned descent to the floor (or extension of the level, such as a trash can or other equipment) with or without injury to the patient. All types of falls are to be included, whether they result from physiological reason (fainting) or from environmental reason (slippery floor). Include assisted falls when a staff member attempts to minimize the impact of the fall (exclude falls by visitors, students, and staff members).

Falls sustained by a toddler during the ordinary course of learning to walk also need to be taken into consideration.[1]

Room Education

Universal fall prevention interventions/low-risk interventions (for all patients admitted to the hospital) include a full assessment of the patient's coordination or balance before assisting with transfer/mobility activities.

Training Family

Patient and family education is advised. Staff need to provide an age-appropriate explanation regarding the fall precautions and educate patients and family/significant others about their responsibility in preventing falls and calling for the team when needed.

---

[1] www.flexmonitoring.org/wp-content/uploads/2013/07/PolicyBrief24_Falls-Prevention.pdf.

Most of the time the family does not think about the fall risks; therefore, informing patient and family/significant other regarding risk factors associated with noncompliance is essential.

High-Risk Prevention

High-risk prevention hospitals need to be mindful of falls and should focus on rules:

1. Initiate top precautions including yellow armbands and double-sided nonslip socks—please note that this is not the admission armband
2. Place a fall icon on the external door and in a prominent location in the patient room to alert staff and family of high fall risk
3. Communicate high fall risk on the patient's whiteboard
4. Out-of-bed assistance mandatory (i.e., do not leave patient unattended while in the restroom; remain at arm's length)
5. Initiate sitter if required in the hospital sitter policy
6. Implement bed or chair alarms (if available), depending upon the patient's location
7. Staff should accompany the patient when ambulating. The patient should not walk alone
8. Assist and monitor a patient using a mobility aid
9. Communicate the patient's fall risk with each handoff
10. Consider the following fall risk–reduction tools when appropriate—floor mat by the bedside, use of gait belt, toilet risers with arms, bathroom lights on at night, and use of shower shoes and shower chair for at-risk patients.

Documentation

If the fall occurs, it is imperative to have a protocol and to provide care as the patient's condition requires.

A general assessment is needed first. Assess the patient's vital signs, level of consciousness, and physical condition before moving the patient. Reassess as required. Notify the physician or designee on call.

The house supervisor or administrator on call needs to be notified together with the family/significant other unless the patient requests nonnotification.

If the family is not available, the staff need to notify the durable power of attorney **if** the person designated to receive information about the patient is confused or incapable of making decisions.

Initiate appropriate fall risk interventions based on assessment and a risk assessment to avoid possible recurrences.

Medical Records

Document the following in the medical record post fall:

1. Circumstances surrounding the fall as known at the time
2. Assessment findings
3. Presence of restraints, if in use
4. Notifications, to whom and time of notification. If applicable, document the patient's request not to inform family/significant other of the fall
5. Patient/family education
6. Care and treatment provided to the patient.

Nursing documentation should include document assessment including patient/family education of the risk of fall. This way of fall occurred A note of the pre- and post-fall interventions will be more appropriate.

Data collection may be paper based and then entered into the event reporting system.

Significant Injury as the Result of a Fall

Falls with significant injury come from risk event of fall; it needs to be avoided at all cost because it can turn into the following outcomes:

■ Amputation
■ Cerebral dysfunction
■ Death
■ Dental damage
■ Disfigurement
■ Dislocation
■ Fracture
■ Hematoma – epidural
■ Hematoma – subdural
■ Hemorrhage
■ Injury to organ/loss of organ
■ Lacerations requiring suturing
■ Wound dehiscence
■ Wound evisceration.

Chapter 30

Hand Hygiene

Hand Hygiene Goals

Hand hygiene is referred to as hand washing, antiseptic hand wipe, antiseptic hand rub, or surgical hand asepsis.[1] The goal of hand hygiene is to remove or destroy the microorganisms on hands.[2]

Hand washing is washing of hands with facility-approved soap and water. Hand hygiene is the most critical action in preventing and controlling infections in healthcare facilities.

Personnel must decontaminate their hands before and after contact with any patient and at the beginning and end of their shift. Staff may carry hospital-provided hand sanitizer in their pockets unless contradicted by the department policy.

From the Premier Safety Institute report, we read: *Hand washing is one of the best ways to stay healthy and avoid getting sick and spreading infections like colds, flu or intestinal infections to others, in any setting, including the home, at work, at school, when traveling, or in a healthcare setting. General hand washing can be done with only soap and water or an alcohol-based hand sanitizer that doesn't even require water*

---

[1] www.cdc.gov/oralhealth/infectioncontrol/faq/hand.htm.
[2] https://quizlet.com/301883173/unit-4-infection-prevention-flash-cards/.

to use. Public health experts are hoping that everyone would adopt the habit of always cleaning hands when preparing food, eating, using the toilet, changing a diaper, or touching a sick or injured person.[3]

Engage Patient and Family

Hand hygiene is for all. We need, therefore, to involve patients, and particularly the patients' family, in observing rules and helping their family members to stay in a clean environment. It is about any person that has contact with a patient's room. It is about patient care and family-centered care.

Why Clean the Hand?

It is the best practice involved in hand hygiene and the hospital-based hand hygiene program.

The Infection Control Today research showed: *Although this aspect of healthcare hand hygiene has been studied minimally, there is cause for concern and a need for more study in this area. In a recent survey which cultured patients' hands after being hospitalized for at least 48 hours on medical-surgical units, 39 percent of patients' hands cultured positive for Clostridium difficile, vancomycin-resistant Enterococcus, methicillin-resistant Staphylococcus aureus, and Acinetobacter. Further studies are planned in this area to clearly define if organisms are present on admission or acquired during the hospitalization. While there is emerging interest in the patient and their environment as potential sources of healthcare-associated infections (HAIs), these studies also highlight the need for healthcare personnel to assist*

---

[3] www.premiersafetyinstitute.org/safety-topics-az/hand-hygiene/hand-hygiene/.

the patient in their hand hygiene. Many patients are unable to open a towelette package, or to reach the alcohol-based hand rub on the wall, or walk to the bathroom to use soap and water after using a bedpan or bedside commode and before eating. There is also a call to action for industry innovators to design patient-friendly hand hygiene products and dispensers so that the patient can clean his hands, or the healthcare personnel can conveniently assist the patient with their hand hygiene needs.[4]

Safeguard Environment

Hand hygiene is the key to safeguarding the patient-care environment. It is as essential for patients and visitors to practice proper hand hygiene as it is for the healthcare professional. Cross-contamination from dirty hands to the patient environment can cause the spread of potentially harmful bacteria. Hand hygiene products should be made accessible to patients and visitors, and steps should be in place to create an environment in which patients feel comfortable asking and reminding their caregivers to sanitize their hands. Also, facilities can provide patient-focused educational materials on hand hygiene and include hand hygiene–specific questions on patient-satisfaction surveys.[4]

Wash hands and use gel. Gel disinfectants should be placed in every room for everyone's use. Physicians and nurses should wash their hands before and after they have contact with patients. Families and others should wash when they go home or when they are in contact with other places on the same floor.

---

[4] www.infectioncontroltoday.com/hand-hygiene/patient-empowerment-hand-hygiene-strategy.

Suggested Reading

1. Istenes NA, Hazelett S, Bingham JE, Kirk J, Abell G, Fleming E. Hand hygiene in healthcare: The role of the patient. *APIC Annual Education Conference and International Meeting* [15–237], Washington, DC, April 27, 2011.
2. Kirk J. GOJO and Global Thought Leaders Share Future of Healthcare Hand Hygiene Compliance at APIC 5/28/2014, http://gojo.com/en/newsroom/blog/2014/GOJO-Global-Thought-Leaders-Compliance-APIC?sc_lang=en
3. Centers for Disease Control and Prevention. 2002;2015, CDC Guidelines for Hand Hygiene in Health-Care Settings. Mortality and Morbidity Weekly (MMWR) 51 (RR-16), www.cdc.gov/mmwr/PDF/rr/rr5115.pdf.
4. Ellingson K. 2012 March, Hand Hygiene: New Frontiers in Messaging and Measurement.

Chapter 31

Time-Out for Better Quality

The Never Event Story

The terrifying medical errors are those involving patients who have undergone surgery on the wrong body part, undergone the incorrect procedure, or had a process intended for another patient. These "wrong site, wrong procedure, wrong patient errors" (WSPEs) are rightly termed never events—errors that should never occur and indicate the underlying severe safety problems, as reported by the Agency for Healthcare Research and Quality.

The same agency reported that *wrong-site surgery may involve operating on the wrong side, as in the case of a patient who had the right side of her vulva removed when the cancerous lesion was on the left, or the wrong body site. One example of surgery on the incorrect site is operating on the wrong level of the spine, a surprisingly common issue for neurosurgeons. A classic case of wrong-patient surgery involved a patient who underwent a cardiac procedure intended for another patient with a similar last name.*[1]

The agency concluded that *The Joint Commission's Universal Protocol to prevent WSPEs after the Root cause analyses of WSPEs consistently reveal communication issues as a prominent underlying factor. The concept of the medical timeout—a planned pause before beginning the procedure to review essential aspects of the process with all involved personnel—was developed to improve communication in the operating room and prevent WSPEs. The Universal Protocol also specifies the use of a timeout before all procedures. Although initially designed for operating room procedures, timeouts are now required before any invasive procedure. Comprehensive efforts to improve surgical safety have incorporated timeout principles into surgical safety checklists; while these checklists have been proven to improve surgical and postoperative safety, the low baseline incidence of WSPEs makes it difficult to establish that a single intervention can reduce or eliminate WSPEs.*[1]

Time-Out

Time-out is the pause immediately before a procedure begins to verify the correct patient, site, laterality/digit/spinal level, and system.

The Universal Protocol is a collective checklist used to create a safe climate for the patient undergoing a procedure. It has three phases:

1. Pre-procedural activities
2. Time-out performed immediately before incision or procedure begins
3. A sign-out after the process before leaving the procedure room or area.

---

[1] https://psnet.ahrq.gov/primers/primer/18/wrong-site-wrong-procedure-and-wrong-patient-surgery.

Steps to Achieve a Better Time-Out

The following steps should be completed before every non-emergent operative or other invasive procedure throughout any facility.

1. In the pre-procedure/preoperative area, a confirmation of the correct site, procedure, and patient will occur
2. In the pre-procedure/preoperative area, the patient will be involved when possible. If the patient is unable to participate, a patient representative will attend
3. The physician/qualified licensed provider (QLP) or another practitioner who is scheduled to perform the intended invasive or surgical procedure, as well as privileged to do so, will mark the process/surgical site before the patient enters the procedure/operating room unless the anatomical location is exempt
4. If a patient refuses site marking, the patient's physician/QLP will review the rationale for site marking as well as the risks and implications for refusing site marking. Alternative trademark will be used
5. All questions and concerns will be resolved before the procedure begins. Team members, and if possible, the patient should agree on the resolution of the identified issue or matter before proceeding
6. A time-out will be performed for all cases, including those not requiring site marking. The time-out is done immediately before beginning the procedure
7. The name and date of birth (DOB) are used to verify a patient's identity
8. If a treatment (e.g., anesthesia block or pre-procedural medication administration such as eye drops) is to be performed, it will be done after the site has been marked in the pre-procedural area where the patient verification has occurred.

All patients who undergo an invasive or surgical procedure involving laterality, digits, or spinal levels will have their surgical site marked.

The practitioner who is ultimately accountable for the procedure and is present when the process is performed will mark the site at or adjacent to the incision site at a location that will remain visible after completion of the skin prep and sterile draping.

A sufficiently permanent marker will be used so that the mark is visible at the beginning of the procedure.

If the patient refuses site marking, the provider reviews the rationale with the patient and the implications for not marking the site. If the patient still refuses, the person responsible for site marking uses an alternative method before proceeding, listed as follows.

Procedures Exempt from Site Marking

1. Single organ procedures unless laterality is pertinent (e.g., right-sided brain tumor would need marking)
2. Interventional cases for which the catheter/instrument insertion is not predetermined and bilateral access may be needed (e.g., central line, port placements, vascular access procedures)
3. Premature infants for whom the mark may cause a permanent tattoo.

Call Time-Out Aloud

The nurse should obtain the following information and call out aloud. Document full procedure name and relevant information such as right, left, or bilateral that involves anatomical sites that have laterality, spinal level, or a specific digit. Pre-procedural verification should be done.

The registered nurse NEEDS to check the following:

1. Correct the spelling of patient's name
2. DOB
3. Procedure to be performed
4. Physician's name
5. Implants required, if known and if applicable
6. Other data necessary for hospital operations
7. Verify the patient's identify using at least two identifiers (name and DOB)
8. Confirm the scheduled procedure as stated by the patient and compare to the schedule and source document such as original order, consent, history and physical, progress notes, or consultative notes
9. Verify the site mark as needed
10. Involve the patient's verbal or visual clues
11. Use a patient representative if the patient is cognitively impaired, incompetent, sedated, incapacitated, or a minor. Use a qualified interpreter service if needed to complete the identifiers
12. Verify the site mark. Stop the process, and clarify any discrepancies in data.

Pre- and Postanesthesia Time-Out

Pause before anesthesia-related procedures to verify correct patient, patient procedure, and right side. Laterality, digit, or spinal level is verified if applicable.

After surgery, a sign-out is done after the procedure has been completed and before the patient is moved to another area. In some cases, the sign-out is done in the same room such as the emergency department. The nurse or healthcare professional uses the below checklist to review:

- Procedure performed was recorded
- Instruments, sponge, and needle counts were correct
- The specimen is labeled correctly
- Any equipment concerns
- Any recovery concerns.

Chapter 32

Setting Up Strategies

Caring Out Loud

Communications is indeed the pinnacle of the relationship with anybody. Issues related to patients' experience can be managed both on the clinical and the nonclinical sides by talking to them more, by communicating better, and by caring for them loud and clear. Patient experience can be improved by cutting out all the apprehension, the uncertainty, and the fear that medical care can elicit. It is also essential to anticipate the needs of the patients and their family members. All of these were included by Jake Poore in the so-called *Caring Out Loud.*[1]

A 2016 study published in the Journal of Medical Practice Management on patient complaints found that about 4% of claims were directly related to their medical treatment. But the remaining 96% were related to poor communication between care team members and patients.[1]

---

[1] www.wecreateloyalty.com/caring-out-loud-the-best-way-to-connect-with-patients/.

Caring Out Loud or describing the process of care can accomplish three things:

1. Answer a question
2. Anticipate a need
3. Calm and reassure an anxious patient.

Personalize your patient's experience by using the patient's preferred name more than once in the visit. Using the preferred name creates a more intimate connection and sets the foundation for a more cordial, personal relationship. Engage in culturally appropriate physical contact, such as a handshake when greeting or a supportive arm to assist with ambulation. At each visit, ask about life events or favorite activities and make a note. On subsequent visits, surprise your patient by bringing up the topic in conversation.

The POD Concepts

As the healthcare industry changed, a new configuration called "On Stage/Off Stage" or the "Patient-Oriented Delivery" (POD) arrangement was developed. The PODs involve teamwork areas and collaboration spaces that promote communication. Some of the many benefits to the PODs are much smaller travel distances for the healthcare employees; patients get a more personalized and intimate feeling during their care, and the open "bullpen" allows for efficient workflow and more flexible examination rooms.[2]

In 2001, studies and research produced findings that indicated that diabetic patients were not showing up for their one-on-one consultations with their physicians for care. These patients arrived at clinics and doctor's offices where the "group

---

[2] www.daviswince.com/2012/how-does-the-patient-centered-medical-home-care-concept-translate-to-healthcare-design-for-architects/.

practice" floor plans still existed in medical facilities and found the care experience to be intimidating and lonely.[2]

Through this investigation, the On Stage/Off Stage pattern evolved. By laying out flexible examination rooms along the most desirable portions of the building, shared doctors' offices on the inside of the clinic, and a centrally located collaboration space, the floor plan allows for smaller square footage clinics that reduce leasing costs and also gives the patients a more comfortable environment to receive care in. Also, in many large hospitals and medical office buildings, numerous PODs exist side by side to create clinics within a clinic.[2]

By developing the POD configuration in medical care facilities, team communication and collaboration can occur more prevalently.[2]

We do not use the POD concept in my clinic; we use the idea of open access clinic. All the rooms can be shared, and different providers can share space, offices, and personnel to make the flow better and the patients seen in perfect time. This can be defined as an open-access clinic.

Open-Access Clinic

All rooms for all physicians and all beds for any patients— medicine or surgery. This is the new concept of healthcare— a unified unit or clinic for all, with nurses and physicians interchanging the rooms according to the type of patients. Many years ago, we had surgical and medical wards; currently, we have medical and surgical wards that are used on a first-come-first-serve basis.

The clinic should be the same—open and available, and not sectorial. The efficient physician will know how to navigate and see more patients; the inefficient physician will see less patients and face problems.

The patients will be seen soon; they do not have to go to different floor or clinics.

Of course, if there is a large subspecialty group, it will work the same way given the fact that they can use the office and therefore the room can be used by different providers of different specialties. But this is not the norm in a small practice or in rural area. In these environments, we need more leaders to apply new concepts, and we need the clinic staff to be open-minded and not closed-minded.

Usually, the less people know, the more information they need since they are afraid of changes.

> *A leader is one who knows the way, goes the way, and shows the way.*
>
> **John C. Maxwell.**

It is essential to be open to the patient, as Mark Twain says: *If you tell the truth you don't have to remember anything.*

If you don't know something, admitting it to the patient is not wrong; it only shows your strength. Quoting Mark Twain again, *I was gratified to be able to answer promptly. And I did. That will make you secure and very much appreciated. It is not about pride, it is about patient care! Said you don't know it is not bad. That will make you secure and very much appreciated. It is not about pride, it is about patient care!*

HEALTHCARE CHANGE OF THINKING

Chapter 33

Changing the
Way We Think

The Health System as an Industry

Health system economics have inflated and deflated in the last 30 years. Some hospitals in the 1980s established an internal agency to regulate their flow and to review the requests for the hospitals' facilities and equipments. State agencies were created to promote and embrace the facility charge. The problem with this plan was that the hospital became an industry with similar settings, and like other companies, the terminology was put toward a service and a product. The product was complicated with many variables such as different ages and different diseases to treat, which made it difficult for hospitals to obtain enough information to make intelligent decisions.

During those years, healthcare paid for the service; therefore, there were a few incentives to control the cost. Some believe that the best way to obtain efficiency might be to design a simple reimbursement system, a system that would encourage healthcare providers to cover the costs when they treat the patients.

By making them share in the values and wastes inefficiency, hospitals tried to implement their new system. Before 1984, most insurance companies paid out through their bill charge, by deducting the discount. Many Medicare and Medicaid plans paid costs. The hospitals reimbursed actual damages and made a commercial profit. The hospitals did not take into consideration that the easiest way to increase profit was a cost-plus contract.

Hospital Health Plans

A significant revolution came with the consolidation of the hospital institute incorporation chains. It was a difficult time for many hospitals and many administrators who had grown accustomed to the autonomy and, in some cases, the lack of accountability of the entire system. The second revolution took place in the 1980s with the introduction of the prospective payment system. Cost reimbursement placed rules on healthcare providers.

In the 1990s, more and more providers assumed an insurance role, bypassing the insurance company contract directly with the employers for the position of comprehensive service. The providers understood the economic risks of insurance because of the market share.

Prospective payment system has placed a limit on global hospital revenues; it has state-by-state payment limits. The only way for hospitals to increase revenue was to capture this operation. Therefore, hospitals started to secure and buyild their own health plans. The hospitals did this by informing employees which physicians they must see to receive the maximum discount and by controlling the hospital admission partners and participating physicians. The second issue for the hospital was cost control. One of the most effective insurance organizations is the Health Maintenance Organization (HMO).

After the Affordable Care Act or Obamacare was signed into law by President Barack Obama, more patients had insurances, but few of them had a primary Medicaid insurance and the physician was not paid well. Therefore, they were compelled to close their practice and look to be hired with various healthcare corporations.

Reimbursement

Cost Reimbursement

In cost reimbursement, payment is made according to the length of stay; therefore, longer hospital stays increase hospital reimbursement.[4] Insurance companies pass on the additional costs to the employer, and they increase the premiums. Rarely do they question the validity of the provider charges. Their employer is more than happy to leave them in the hospital longer. Eventually, the patients have to pay the bill through higher premiums.

Capitation System

The first HMO in the country was formed in the 1940s by an industrialist named Eric Keiser. He had the contract to build ships for the war effort. To recruit employees without violating wage control, he began offering his employees health benefits. His program used a prospective payment system called the capitation payment system. The capitation payment system is the one in which the healthcare provider receives a fixed amount per patient per month to provide specific services. The doctor gets this manual, regardless of whether the patient needs the assistance or not. Therefore, it provides an incentive to keep the patient well. If the patient becomes ill, it encourages the physician to use the most cost-effective resources to heal them. Capitation payment does not provide an incentive for the physician to overutilize products and services.

What prevents the physician from providing the cure or the service? This is another issue that needs to be understood. The length of stay is critical, given that the physician can lose money if the patient's visit is too long. Physicians and hospitals might receive HMO bonuses at the end of the year that depend on their savings in hospitalization.

With viable management wanting to prevent losses under the capitation payment, they must help with the type of medicine provided by the prime physician at the hospital, the number of cancer cases treated on an inpatient and outpatient basis, the average time to detect treatable diseases, the average length of hospital stay, mortality rates, etc.

Payments

What types of payments are there today? A kind of debt is the prospective payment system. The diagnosis-related group is a form of potential payment under capitation. Under capitation payment, the hospital sees the fixed amount per hour, per month, regardless of the service rendered.

Quality Crisis in Medicine: Changing the Way We Think

How does the hospital make money? Good contacts with HMOs, localization, and an emphasis on prevention. The capitation payment system was used to prevent the physician from providing unnecessary care. HMOs, with precertification, control the utilization. They instruct the physician how to take care of the patient. Therefore, HMOs try to control the quality of care. How can we prove the physician's decision? I do not know the answer. What I do know is that the HMO's control creates a state of panic. Instead of achieving a better quality of care, they tend to push physicians to see more patients to increase their revenues, since the payment for single patients is now "miserable." Hospitals have the same problem; causing the employees to be laid off. Nurses are now in charge of the care of 12 patients, instead of 6–8 patients. If this system is not adjusted, healthcare will become a low-quality system. We understand the concept of cost containment, but cutting costs will make everyone work more efficiently, and more patients will be seen per hour. Is this what we want when we retire and need healthcare? Many students enrolling in medical school believe it is too much work and that the hours are too long when a mid- to low-level manager's salary is comparable to theirs, even with only 4 years of college.

Focus on Quality

The sole focus should be on quality. That is where the health industry is today. Several factors emphasize quality including:

1. employees' concerns regarding having their physician and hospital choice mandated by their employers
2. increased access to health information through the internet
3. procedures having an improvement in products through total quality management and continuous quality improvement.

Where do we obtain this information to plot in a percentage form to conform to the standard of care?

1. Medical records
2. Business office
3. Physician's office
4. Hospital.

Fraud Prevention

Federal laws governing Medicare fraud and abuse include all of the following:

- False Claims Act
- Anti-Kickback Statute
- Physician Self-Referral Law (Stark Law).

Other scrutinized situations in healthcare are the following:

- False Claims Reward Referrals
- Aberrant Billing
- Upcoding Deficient Documentation & Anti-kickback Statute Buying Beneficiary IDs
- Unneeded Supplies Self-referrals
- Excessive Charges.[1]

New Era

We are now in an era where health care has changed so much that it requires new expertise. The physician is a manager, and one of their goals is to find good employees who understand the job since reimbursement and billing depend on them. Despite this, we should never lose focus on the quality of care.

Suggested Reading

1. Buckingham M, Coffman C. *First Break All the Rules*. Simon and Schuster; 1999.
2. Bolman L, Deal T. *Reframing Organization*. Jossey and Bass; 1997. https://www.emergingrnleader.com/first-break-all-the-rules/

---

[1] Medicare Learning Network, https://go.cms.gov/mln-fraud-abuse.

3. Jones G, George J, Hill C. *Contemporary Management.* Irwin Mc Graw-Hill; 2000. https://trove.nla.gov.au/work/4053759
4. McDermott R, Stock K. *Code Blue.* Traemus Book; 2002. https://www.abebooks.com/book-search/title/code-blue-health-sciences-edition/author/richard-mcdermott/
5. Frezza EE. *The Health Care Collapse.* New York: Routledge Publishing; 2018.
6. Frezza EE. *The Business of Surgery.* Norwalk, CT: CineMed Publishing; 2008.

Chapter 34

Physical Wellness

Maintain Healthy Lifestyles

Much of the information is based on theories and models used by researchers to study the factors associated with healthy living.

There are widely accepted theories and models of behavior change. We need to be aware of the basic principles.

Many adults want to make healthy lifestyle changes but find it difficult to incorporate them. To understand the factors that contribute to making this difficult, it is essential to understand the definition of a "lifestyle."[1]

A useful definition of lifestyle is as follows: *Lifestyles are the behaviors that we adopt based on the context of our life circumstances.*

The Stages of Change is a model developed by Dr. James Prochaska that explains the processes people go through in changing their behaviors. It was initially designed to describe *the stages people use to change negative behaviors such as smoking but has recently been extended to help explain stages of exercise behavior.*[2]

---

[1] www.ecnmag.com/article/2011/08/patient-prepping.

[2] Prochaska JO, DiClemente CC, Norcross JC. In search of how people change: Applications to addictive behaviors. *Am Psychol* 1992;47(9):1102–14.

People are not interested in exercise programs, and hence, efforts at motivating them will probably fall on deaf ears. Individuals in need are beginning to think about starting, but do not know where to start. Initial steps at beginning a regular exercise program need to be taken.[3]

HELP Yourself

The HELP philosophy provides the basis for making a healthy lifestyle change possible. The acronym, HELP, characterizes an integral part of the philosophy: **H**ealth is available to **E**veryone for a **L**ifetime and it is **P**ersonal. Physical activity is not just for athletes; it is for all people. The reason it is essential to adopt and sustain healthy habits early in life is that it *will increase long-term health, wellness, and fitness. It does take each to take personal responsibility for learning and using these skills. Health is more than freedom from illness, disease, and debilitating conditions — the individual needs to take in consideration that every single one of them is unique. Each person's characteristics influence health and wellness. We all have personal limitations and strengths. Some dimensions that involve health-related physical fitness are body composition, muscular endurance, strength, power, cardiorespiratory endurance, and flexibility. A fit person has a relatively low, but not too low, percentage of body fat.*

A healthy person can repeat the movement for an extended period without undue fatigue. Strength varies from person to person because even though you might have the same fit bodies, one person may be able to lift more than the other. Having a robust cardiorespiratory endurance will allow the heart, blood vessels, blood, and the respiratory system to supply nutrients and oxygen to the muscles and give them the ability to utilize fuel to allow sustained exercises[4] [2].

---

[3] https://quizlet.com/77259058/mid-term-concepts-flash-cards/.
[4] Frezza EE. *Kill Your Diet. A Nutrition, Wellness and Exercise Manual.* Cure Your Practice ed. ISBN 9781073475476.

Making Lifestyle Changes

Lifestyle changes are hard to make. Some examples include those who believe that physical activity is important but do not get enough exercise to attain good health.

1. Those who have tried numerous times to lose weight but have failed
2. Those who know what to eat, but they don't do it
3. Those who feel stress regularly, and they do not have a way out.

Changes in lifestyles are frequently desired but often not accomplished. Lifestyle changes occur in at least *five different stages*:

1. The pre-contemplation stage is where a person decides that they will never change
2. The contemplation stage is when the person is thinking about a change
3. The preparation stage is the stage where they are getting ready to make a lifestyle change
4. The action stage is where changes have already been made
5. The maintenance stage is where the person regularly practices healthy lifestyle.

Learning self-management skills can alter factors that lead to healthy lifestyles changes.

Self-planning is a particularly important self-management skill. *There are six steps*:

1. Clarifying reasons
2. Identifying needs
3. Setting personal goals
4. Selecting program components
5. Writing a plan
6. Evaluating progress.

Implementing Behavioral Changes

There are *six steps* that are required for implementing behavioral changes.

1. Planning. Common reasons for following a diet are to improve personal appearance, lose weight, and increase energy levels. Before moving on to step two, you must reflect on your reasons for wanting to make lifestyle changes

2. Building on your strengths and overcoming weaknesses. With practice, self-assessments become more accurate; this is the reason it is essential to repeat self-assessments and pay close attention to the procedures when performing them

3. Explaining why goals are more specific than rights. Establishing particular things that you want to can provide a basis for feedback that your program is working. Short-term goals take days or weeks to achieve. Long-term goals take longer to achieve, sometimes months or even years. There are also general goals that are broad statements of your reasons for wanting to achieve something—for example, changing behavior such as eating better or being more active or losing weight or maintaining fitness. Smart goals are less general and have several important aspects. Quick goals are specific, measurable, attainable, realistic, and timely

4. Including the specific program components that will meet their needs and goals, which include meal plans for nutrition and specific activities for their physical activity plan

5. Putting your plan in writing. This establishes your intentions and increases your chances of adherence

6. Self-monitoring is an excellent way to assess success in meeting behavioral goals.

Enabling Factors

■ Goal-setting skills
■ Self-assessment skills
■ Self-monitoring skills
■ Self-planning skills
■ Performance skills
■ Adopting coping skills
■ Learning consumer skills
■ Managing time.

One of the most crucial reinforcing elements is success. If you change a behavior and experience success, this makes you want to keep doing a behavior! Research also suggests that it is desirable to promote autonomy and freedom of choice so that change is self-directed.

Reinforcing Factors

■ Building on successes
■ Finding social support
■ Preventing relapse.

Suggested Reading

1. Charles C, Welk G, Corbin W, Welk K. *Concept of Fitness and Wellness*. McGraw Hill; 2016.
2. Eldo Frezza E, Mariah Dutchover , Shyla Ervin , Joshua Watson , Jordan Hendricks , Celina Lavadie , Eleazar Maslian , Kemberly Mendoza , Jamie Stuart , Natalia Vital. 2017. Fighting Obesity: The Benefit of Diet and Exercise for High School Students, https://gavinpublishers.com/articles/Editorial/Journal-of-Obesity-and-Nutritional-Disorders/Fighting-Obesity-The-Benefit-of-Diet-and-Exercise-for-High-School-Students.

Chapter 35

Circle of Support

First, I would like to address the difference between the mean-
ings of "circle of support" and "circle of health support."

Circle of Support

The most important circle of support comes from family and
friends who help in the patient's experiences. Patient-centered
care is depicted as follows:

Patients

Physicians

Medical offices

Hospitals

Healthcare support system

The factors mentioned that are of utmost importance in reaching your support system is depicted below.

Changing your lifestyle for a healthy body requires social support. One example is binge eating for which you need assistance. Social support comes from your family, friends, coworkers, classmates, teachers, or other people who are attached to you. The best social support you will ever have is the presence of your family and friends because they will not only cheer you, but they will also join your fight and help reach your goal. This social support helps you to have a positive outlook in achieving goals; it can also assist in having a close relationship with your family and friends. I recommend having a partner in overcoming your purpose of having a healthy body. It thus helps fight mental illness and helps to have a positive mind.

A Circle of Support

The components of the circle of support are depicted below.

Eating healthy
Regular exercise
Support system
Regular checkup
Regular vaccinations: flu, herpes zoster, etc.
Family
Children
Significant others
Spirituality
Decrease risk-taking
Reduce stress

A circle of support is sometimes called a circle of friends. The circle was developed to support individuals to become connected in the community and to make friendships and relationships. The circle is a natural process for most of us; when we are troubled or happy, we call on our family and friends to share our pain or joy and to help us think through what we can do. For people who are disempowered, such as people with learning disabilities, this does not happen.[1]

The individuals and/or the family may become isolated. This is the time they need a circle of friends/support to develop around them.

This can be as simple as a group of people who meet together to help somebody with the problems of their life or simply keep them company. It can be about expanding their social circle, their friends, visiting another side of the family.

Those with more significant needs will usually require support from their family or someone who knows them well to ensure the circle meetings are run and maintained. Circles can be as small or as large as required.

To develop a circle, a relationship map is created with the individual to identify the people in their life. Family members are invited to look at who could be brought into the circle. This commitment is unpaid, as "friendship" should not constitute a paid relationship.[1]

Mapping Your Support

A map of people close to the patients is needed to define the support system and their circle. The circle is requested to make connections with other people. These new connections are nurtured, and eventually, others are invited to join the circle of friends.

---

[1] www.mentalhealth.org.uk/learning-disabilities/a-to-z/c/circles-support-and-circles-friends.

Planning

Circles bring a group of people together, to meet regularly to identify and achieve patients' goals. It is a partnership and a commitment made to the person by the closest people and their support system.

Workplace

Circles of support in the workplace can be beneficial to ensure that the person is well supported to do their work independently.[1]

Holistic Circle

Beginning with a comprehensive definition in ancient times, the official American description of health now focuses on physical health and disease symptoms. This limited definition of health is an inadequate foundation for holistic healthcare strategies. The model includes concepts of balance, energy systems, and mind–body integration from non-Western health practices. A holistic definition of health suggests an expanded range of positive health behaviors. The visual representation of the model can be used by healthcare professionals and clients to identify disease-reduction strategies or health improvement programs for competent individuals. Understanding and expanding the conceptualization of health and health improvement strategies offer the possibility of improving client satisfaction and health status outcomes.[2]

---

[2] Saylor C. The circle of health: A health definition model. *J Holist Nurs* 2004;22(2):97–115.

A New Support Building

The new support building approach has proved to be a useful tool in assisting stakeholders in exploring health system changes in a patient-centric approach.

The goal of patient care is to manage the health of the populations. The building is based on demonstrating improved outcomes and quality that will then enhance the patient experience.

Unfortunately, there are many challenges faced by hospitals and health systems today. It is not easy to ensure success from pre- and post-care on patients during and after a hospital visit, and these are critical to success construction of your new support building. The following are the issues that most commonly affect daily patient health:

1. *Population Health:* Manage large populations and address gaps in care
2. *Fee-for-Service:* Increase efficiency, drive growth
3. *Alternative Payment Models:* Contain costs, enhance quality, and improve outcomes
4. *Improved Patient Experience:* Improve patient satisfaction ratings.

Portals

Health Patient Portal should be built for care access. These portals need to be confidential, with private information protected. Authorized users should be defined by giving the opportunity to an approved family member to access the Health Patient Portal. This can be personalized by providing convenient access to hospital test results and medical records.[3]

---

[3] www.lowellgeneral.org/patients-and-visitors/for-patients/patient-portal.

Chapter 36

Difficult Patients

Refusing Treatment

The first medical ethics principles of the American Medical Association[1] mentioned that physicians should be able to refuse treatment except in emergency.

Unfortunately, both the physician and the nurse are under continuous pressure to provide beyond medical care despite what the patient does.

Most professionals believe that the drastic step of refusing to operate on a patient should be taken only as the last resort except in emergency.

According to Wikipedia: *In the United States, the total number of stays discharged against medical advice (AMA) discharged increased 41 percent between 1997 and 2011. For adults ages 45–64 years, the percentage of AMA discharges increased from 27 percent in 1997 to 41 percent in 2011. By payer, the share of AMA discharges increased from 25 percent to 29 percent for Medicare and decreased from 21 percent to 16 percent for private insurance.*[2]

---

[1] www.ama-assn.org/sites/ama-assn.org/files/corp/media-browser/code-of-medical-ethics-chapter-2.pdf.

[2] https://en.wikipedia.org/wiki/Against_medical_advice.

The available data suggest that in general, patients discharged Against Medical Advice (AMA) have an increased risk of hospital readmission and potentially death. Patients discharged AMA, even though the risk and benefit are explained to the patient.

While most practitioners believe that the AMA discharge form is needed to limit liability on the part of the medical facility in case there are complications, it is an invalid assumption and may lead to coercive practices that do not support patients.

There is also a *widespread ethical consensus that even when patients decline recommended treatment, health care professionals still have a duty to care for and support patients.*[2] But if the patient does not want to, if they challenge you, or if they are aggressive and abusive?

How Patients Become Abusive

The following are the reasons or circumstances for patients to become abusive.

- Patients are under the influence of drugs and alcohol
- After psychiatric trauma, patients can be unpredictable with both verbal and physical outbursts
- Crowded waiting rooms
- Long waiting times can cause tempers to flare and people's patience to wear quite thin
- In general, patients' insecurities, anxieties, and fears may surface in the form of verbal or physical abuse
- The department should have a plan in place that includes readily available security personnel, alarm buttons within easy reach, and a security committee dedicated to creating a safe working environment[3]

---

[3] www.coursehero.com/file/p3m2lbt/abuse-due-to-individuals-feeling-as-if-their-needs-are-not-being-met-or-they/.

■ Your patients' actions reflect their feelings and experiences, and outside issues, not you, are at the root of their behavior.

Avoid Getting Too Close to Patients

Getting close to patients can appear to be a positive attitude, but can turn against you. According to a recent study, unhealthy boundaries could be[4]:

1. Sharing intimate personal life with patients
2. Keeping personal secrets with patients
3. Receiving gifts from patients
4. Speaking to the patient about your own problems
5. Speak poorly about coworkers or the hospital to patients
6. Talking to patients/families about things that are out of your scope of practice
7. Giving certain patients extra time or attention
8. Give patients personal contact information or money
9. Failing to set limits with a patient
10. Spending personal time with patients when on duty
11. Feeling you are better than your team.[5]

What Is the Best Approach?

Set firm boundaries and insist that you be treated with respect, just as you are treating them with respect.

■ Allow the patient to tell you why they are acting as they are
■ Give them a chance for their fears and frustrations to be heard

---

[4] www.nursingtermpapers.com/identify-and-explore-the-patients-needs-and-problems-help-to-develop-the-patients-strengths-and-new-coping-skills/.
[5] www.nursetogether.com.

- Analyze and assess the reasons for their anger, and use calm, reassuring logic to help them overcome their anxieties
- Address unanswered questions[3]
- Regular testing of panic buttons and the planned response to them is vital
- Liaison with local police and have protocols for circumstances in which police should be called
- Control loud noises and staff rushing about that can exacerbate tense situations.

Recommended Communication Strategies

The recommended communication strategies toward patients include the following.

- Trying to be positive
- Offering the patient something rather than refusing outright
- Treating the aggressive patient with a team approach rather than entering into arguments
- Respecting the dignity of all patients.

Recommended Organization Features

The recommended organization features include the following:

- More than one receptionist on at all times to have a backup in case of need
- Established routines for unlocking and locking up premises at the beginning or end of the day
- Being able to communicate quickly but discreetly with doctors during surgery to alert the doctor about an aggressive patient.[6]

---

[6] www.nntlmc.co.uk.

Firing a Patient

According to the Texas Medical Association, *The essence of the physician-patient relationship is the physician's agreement, in response to an overt or implied request, to become responsible for the patient's care. The link is not dependent on the fact of whether the patient pays the physician money for services rendered. If that were true, then no charity care provided to a person would result in the formation of a physician-patient relationship. The same is true for unpaid fees: failure to pay does not automatically terminate the relationship. However, it may be the case that the patient's persistent refusal of interfering with the physician's ability to deliver appropriate medical care. One cannot expect the physician to continue providing uncompensated care and believe that his attitude towards the patient will remain unaffected unless one has chosen to regard a particular patient as a charity case. In that case, it may be justifiable to terminate the physician-patient relationship so long as the other steps outlined here are followed.*

So long as the physician-patient relationship is established and not definitively terminated, a physician owes the patient the same duty of care. Otherwise, there is a danger of abandonment (or at least a successful liability claim based on delay in treatment).

We need to remember that medical malpractice law holds physicians to a higher standard of care than an ordinary business person because physicians have historically held themselves to a higher level of conduct. Thus a person is a patient for all purposes regardless of their pay status until the relationship is terminated.

There is a question of whether the patient, by leaving "against medical advice" intended to discharge their physician. The splitting of the hospital could have occurred due to facts unrelated to the physician-patient relationship or medical treatment.[7]

To be noted that if the physician–patient relationship has not been terminated by the acts of either party, there is still an obligation to the patient.[7]

---

[7] https://tma.custhelp.com/ci/fattach/get/18682/0/filename/Physician+Patient+Term ination+and+Sample+Letter.pdf.

Chapter 37

Psychological Support, Depression, and Suicide

Psychological support has become a pressing issue in healthcare. More patients appear to suffer from depression or other problems that require psychological help. The system has been overwhelmed by the need for psychological assistance from all over the world, ranging from the victims of mass shootings to soldiers returning from wars. The veterans administration (VA) has been struggling to find psychologists to be hired in the system.

Traditional Support System for Psychological Issues

The traditional support systems for psychological issues are listed below:

- Social workers
- Pastors
- Family members
- Friends.

But unfortunately, this is not sufficient anymore since the complexity of the psychological diseases has been difficult even for professionals, nothing less for family and friends.

A good system adopted in Europe is the utilization of caregivers available to visit patients and families, and some to sleep and stay 24 h with the patients at home to avoid delay visit at the hospitals and clinic.

In the United States, this system is difficult and expensive. In Europe, patients receive support from the health insurance and the social system, thus leaving only minimal expenses for the family.

I have had a very good experience with this system— the caregiver coming home to take care of my father who suffered from Alzheimer's was a great help and a key to his care.

Current Requirements

Nowadays, the system is looking for:

- Psychologists
- Psychiatrists
- More facilities specialized in mental health
- Specialized caregivers
- Home health specialized
- Psychological rehab facilities.

Shortage of Psychologists

An estimated 106,500 psychologists are licensed in the United States. California (17,890), New York (12,020), and Pennsylvania (5,620) have the most licensed psychologists, while Wyoming (170), South Dakota (190), and Alaska (190) have the fewest.

The District of Columbia (173.3) and Vermont (100.5) have the highest representation of licensed psychologists per 100,000 population, while Mississippi (11.9) and South Carolina (13.0) have the lowest.[1]

More than 50% of Americans are known to face[2] mental health challenges. These are:

- depression
- anxiety
- suicidal thoughts
- substance abuse
- grief over a loss
- trouble adjusting to a life change.

The Center for Disease Control (CDC) reports that 43.4 million adults suffered from some behavioral health issue in 2015 alone.

There are no enough psychiatrists or psychologists to go around and not even a social worker or a case manager to take care of them, particularly in rural communities.[2]

According to a new study in the *American Journal of Preventive Medicine*,[3] a majority of nonmetropolitan counties (65%) do not have a psychiatrist, and almost half of the nonmetropolitan counties (47%) do not have a psychologist.[4]

Poor access to mental healthcare, according to experts, is a severe issue that is almost as bad if not more than those linked to drug abuse and suicide.

---

[1] www.apa.org/monitor/2014/06/datapoint.aspx.

[2] www.simplemost.com/why-theres-a-severe-shortage-of-mental-health-professionals-in-rural-areas/.

[3] www.wral.com/there-s-a-severe-shortage-of-mental-health-professionals-in-rural-areas-here-s-why-that-s-a-serious-problem/17640716/.

[4] www.wmal.com/2018/06/22/theres-a-severe-shortage-of-mental-health-professionals-in-rural-areas-heres-why-thats-a-serious-problem/.

The Washington Post reported a Merritt Hawkins, a physician search firm, study *which found that searches for psychiatrists this past year were the highest than at any time in its 27-year history, according to a recent report. Psychiatrists trailed only primary care doctors on the list of the firm's 20 most in-demand medical specialties.*[5]

From the same article, we read: *States with the highest rates of mental illness and the lowest rates of access to care are in the South and the West, according to the patient advocacy group Mental Health America. Rural areas face some of the most significant deficits. The lack of psychiatrists and other mental-health providers is part of an overall shortage of physicians in the United States. Earlier this year, a study by the Association of American Medical Colleges concluded that the nation would face a deficit of between 46,000 and 90,400 doctors within a decade. While primary care doctors will certainly be in short supply, it said, the most significant deficiencies may be among specialist physicians who care for the elderly, including psychiatrists.*[6]

What Are We Talking About?

Alcoholism

Alcohol abuse can destroy both family and personal life of a person.

People who drink are dangerous to themselves as well as to others, and also impair the health and happiness of the people they love. Sixty to seventy percent of relationship breakups are secondary to abuse, and among these is alcohol abuse.[7]

---

[5] www.washingtonpost.com/news/to-your-health/wp/2015/10/22/why-its-so-hard-to-find-a-mental-health-professional/.

[6] www.washingtonpost.com/news/to-your-health/wp/2015/10/22/why-its-so-hard-to-find-a-mental-health-professional/?noredirect=on&utm_term=.b5d5ead5393d.

[7] https://americanaddictioncenters.org/alcoholism-treatment/family-marital-problems.

Drug Addictions

Drug addiction is a disease that affects your brain and behavior. People cannot resist the urge to use them, no matter how much harm the drugs may cause. As specified in WebMD, *Drug addiction isn't about just heroin, cocaine, or other illegal drugs. You can get addicted to alcohol, nicotine, opioid painkillers, and other legal substances.*[8]

Suicide

Suicide is a serious public health problem. The fact is that deaths are preventable with timely interventions. Therefore, we need a national suicide prevention strategy to apply to this problem.

From the victims' perspective, suicide is seen as a permanent solution to temporary troubles. Life's difficulties are hard to take and they can push people over the edge. The survivors of attempted suicide mostly express relief that their attempts failed. Nowadays suicidal thoughts arise in people of all ages, even young adults, and the numbers are rising.[9]

Suicide Facts and Figures

According to Elizabeth Lee Vliet, *Physicians, in general, have a higher rate of death than other professional groups and the public. Women physicians' suicide rates are reported to be up to 400% higher than women in other professions. Male physicians' rates are 50% to 70% higher.*[10]

---

[8] www.webmd.com/mental-health/addiction/drug-abuse-addiction.

[9] https://counselingcenter.utk.edu/self-help-materials/the-issue-of-suicide/.

[10] Physician Suicide Rates Have Climbed Since Obamacare, https://physiciansnews. com/2015/05/19/physician-suicide-rates-have-climbed-since) (https://www. certapet.com/emotional-support-animals-and-mental-health/.

- It is the seventh leading cause of death among U.S. men
- It is the fifth leading cause of death among U.S. women
- It is the third leading cause of death for Americans aged 15–24 years
- Most prevalent in elderly and adolescents
- Highest rate: in men over 85
- Physician health experts say as many as 400 U.S. physicians take their lives each year
- Major depressive disorder (MDD) affects 13%–17% of Americans every year
- The rate of MDD in physicians is like that of the general population: 13% of male physicians and 20% of female physicians
- One-third of medical residents have a diagnosable MDD during residency
- About 30% of physicians show MDD one year after graduation
- MDD is a risk factor for suicide
- Physicians who make suicide attempts are much more likely to complete suicide than non-physicians
- The rate of death in male physicians is 70% higher, whereas in the case of female physicians it is 250%–400% higher than the general population.

Depression

The psychiatric association defines depression as a frequent and severe *medical illness that negatively affects how you feel, the way you think and how you act. Fortunately, it is also treatable. Depression causes feelings of sadness and a loss of interest in activities once enjoyed. It can lead to a variety of emotional and physical problems and can decrease a person's ability to function at work and home.*[11]

---

[11] www.psychiatry.org/patients-families/depression/what-is-depression.

Depression symptoms can include:

■ Feeling sad
■ Having a depressed mood
■ Loss of interest in activities
■ Changes in appetite
■ Trouble sleeping
■ Sleeping too much
■ Loss of energy
■ Increased fatigue
■ Increase in purposeless physical activity
■ Slowed movements and speech
■ Feeling worthless
■ Guilty
■ Difficulty thinking
■ Difficult making decisions
■ Suicidal ideation.

From the same organization, we have learned that *Symptoms must last at least two weeks for a diagnosis of depression. Thyroid problems, a brain tumor or vitamin deficiency, can give similar symptoms. Depression affects an estimated one in 15 adults (6.7%) in any given year. And one in six people (16.6%) will experience depression at some time in their life. Depression can strike at any time, but on average, first appears during the late teens to mid-20s. Women are more likely than men to experience depression. Some studies show that one-third of women will undergo a major depressive episode in their lifetime.*[11]

Seeking Treatment

Mental health professionals should be consulted such as psychiatrists, clinical psychologists, and master's-level therapists. Unfortunately, some patients may first seek help from a general physician or a religious counselor. It is wise to find relief even when signs are not critical to help prevent depression from getting worse.[11]

Most severe cases of depression respond to antidepressant medications. Other types of mood disorders require specific treatments and drugs such as bipolar or schizophrenia.

Individual psychotherapy, alone or in combination with medication, can work well. The cognitive and behavioral approach, group therapy, is useful in treating depressive symptoms and raising insights about the self and the relationships with others.[11]

Depressed individuals who are at high risk of killing themselves need to be hospitalized. It is not the end of the world or such a drastic measure if we think that this can save lives and allow the person to get the treatment and support that they need.[12]

---

[12] https://caps.ucsc.edu/resources/depression.html.

Chapter 38

Respecting Patients' Choices and Autonomy

Autonomy

The concept of autonomy first came into prominence in ancient Greece (from the Greek *auto-nomos*), where it characterized self-governing city-states. In the European Renaissance, autonomy came to be accepted as a property of persons. Today, the concept is used in both senses, although most contemporary philosophers deal with in-depth pendency primarily as a property of persons.[1]

Doctors respect the autonomy of patients by treating patients with dignity and respect and involving them in their care.

Patient choice is essential and comes not only by simplifying caring for them but also by respecting their autonomy.[2] The inherent value of patient choice lies not only in the decision itself but also in the process by which the determination is made.

---

[1] https://tma.custhelp.com/ci/fattach/get/18682/0/filename/Physician+Term ination+and+Sample+Letter.pdf.

[2] https://abetternhs.net/2011/09/29/point/.

Laura Seding reported: *Expressing respect for patients' autonomy means acknowledging that patients who have decision-making capacity have the right to make decisions regarding their care, even when their decisions contradict their clinicians' recommendations.[3] The idea of "informed consent" is a hallmark of Western medical ethics that came about following the horrors recounted in the Nuremberg trials and was codified in American law through Canterbury v. Spence in 1972 [3]. It requires physicians to respect patients' autonomy by giving them the information needed to understand the risks and benefits of a proposed intervention, as well as the reasonable alternatives to an independent decision.[3]*

The same author reminded us that *Family members can undoubtedly coerce, persuade, or manipulate a patient. Focusing on the strict definition of autonomy and failing to recognize an individual as part of a family leads to an incomplete understanding of decision making for informed consent.[4]*

Freedom of Choices

Respecting yourself means giving and defining self-respect. Physicians start doing that by listening to the patient's point of view truly. We may not always agree with one another on every topic (and you should never adopt a point of view with which you do not agree), but we should allow patients to have and express their opinions—regardless of whether we agree with them or not.

---

[3] https://journalofethics.ama-assn.org/article/whats-role-autonomy-patient-and-family-centered-care-when-patients-and-family-members-dont.

[4] Sedig L. What's the role of autonomy in patient- and family-centered care when patients and family members don't agree? *AMA J Ethics*, www.ncbi.nlm.nih.gov/pubme26854631.

Confucius

According to Confucius, religion is necessary for any society in addition to religious tolerance in a pluralistic society. There is a reasonable definition of what an established religion is and that organized religious practices are not inherently evil. All patients need to be treated with respect and understanding by supporting their individual choices in treatment and religion. Therefore, the healthcare provider needs to establish dialogue between caregiver and patient/relative to meet their goals. It is always advisable to talk with the patient about their needs. The patient may also be able to provide a contact number for their spiritual advisor. If the patient is mentally competent and of age, we need to respect their choices unless they pose a threat to self or others.

Hippocrates

As in our Hippocratic Oath, we swear "first, do no harm," which is still valid for all and protects the current as well as potential patients.

Only in a situation of emergency or danger is the patient allowed to change the decision and a two-physician consent is permitted.

The Hippocratic Oath stated: *I will use treatment to help the sick according to my ability and judgment, but I will never use it to injure or wrong them.* The oath obliges the physician, based on his ability and judgment, to benefit the patient. This is the principle of beneficence.[5] The oath also places on the physician the obligation not to harm the patient (*"premium no nuocere"*). This is the principle of nonmaleficence.

---

[5] https://sites.sju.edu/icb/hippocratic-oath-autonomy/

Immanuel Kant

The most influential philosopher in the arena of personal freedom was Immanuel Kant (*Groundwork of the Metaphysics of Morals* (Grundlegung zur Metaphysik der Sitten), 1785; *Critique of Practical Reason* (Kritik der praktischen Vernunft), 1788; *The Metaphysics of Morals* (Metaphysik der Sitten), 1797) who believed that: *all persons are owed respect just because they are persons, that is, free rational beings. To be a person is to have a status and worth that is unlike that of any other kind of being. The only response that is appropriate to such a being is respect.*

In Kant's theory of value, dignity is valued morally above all other entities. Kant argues that rational beings are the only entities that end in themselves and that all intelligent people are therefore ends in themselves.[6]

The capacity for autonomy, according to Kant, is the basis of the dignity of human and every rational nature; and by this rational nature, is an end in itself. Kant grounded dignity of persons (and respect for persons generally) in our capacity for autonomy.

Aristotle

The Greek philosopher Aristotle (384–322 B.C.)[7] contributes to nearly every aspect of human knowledge, from logic to biology to ethics and aesthetics. In Arabic philosophy, he was known only as "The First Teacher"; in the West, he was "The Philosopher."

According to Aristotle[5:] *Respect is the acknowledgment in attitude and conduct of the dignity of persons as ends in themselves. Respect for such beings is not only appropriate*

---

[6] https://plato.stanford.edu/entries/respect
[7] www.history.com/topics/ancient-history/aristotle

but also morally and unconditionally required: the status and worth of persons is such that they must always be respected, which is the supreme principle of morality, commands that our actions express due respect for the value of persons.

Index